Praise fo

"Jiulio's book is the most _____ ever read on how to employ the chakras—and stillness—to awaken to the wholeness already within. His logic is sheer poetry, and the practices are wondrous."

—**CYNDI DALE,** bestselling author of *Llewellyn's Complete Book of Chakras*

"*Your Inner Healer* is abundant with spiritual insights, guided healing meditations, and self-love practices that will help you light your own path to wellness."

—**AMY B. SCHER,** bestselling author of *How to Heal Yourself When No One Else Can*

YOUR Inner Healer

About the Author

Jiulio Consiglio (Ontario, Canada) is a spiritual teacher and author who focuses on the transformative power of inner stillness, the mind-body-spirit connection, and psychic abilities development. His message is that there is life beyond fear and incessant thinking and it is found in the dimension of inner stillness. Jiulio is the author of *Open Your Third Eye* and a contributor to *Finding Your Calm* and offers his consciousness-based teachings to individuals and groups. Visit him at www.JiulioConsiglio.com.

YOUR
Inner
Healer

Using Chakras and Energy Medicine to
ACHIEVE WHOLENESS

JIULIO CONSIGLIO

LLEWELLYN
WOODBURY, MINNESOTA

FIRST EDITION
First Printing, 2025

Book design by Samantha Peterson
Cover design by Kevin R. Brown
Editing by Stephanie Finne
Interior illustrations by Llewellyn Art Department

Llewellyn Publications is a registered trademark of Llewellyn Worldwide Ltd.

Library of Congress Cataloging-in-Publication Data (Pending)
ISBN: 978-0-7387-7897-6

Llewellyn Worldwide Ltd. does not participate in, endorse, or have any authority or responsibility concerning private business transactions between our authors and the public.

All mail addressed to the author is forwarded but the publisher cannot, unless specifically instructed by the author, give out an address or phone number.

Any internet references contained in this work are current at publication time, but the publisher cannot guarantee that a specific location will continue to be maintained. Please refer to the publisher's website for links to authors' websites and other sources.

Llewellyn Publications
A Division of Llewellyn Worldwide Ltd.
2143 Wooddale Drive
Woodbury, MN 55125-2989
www.llewellyn.com

Printed in the United States of America

Other Books by Jiulio Consiglio

Finding Your Calm (Contributor)

Open Your Third Eye

This book is dedicated to all those who are on the spiritual path, who have the desire to grow, evolve, and make the return to wholeness. May you remember that what you seek is already within you. And may you come to experience the healing, clarity, wisdom, strength, and understanding of inner stillness on your journey, for you are all needed to shine your light brightly at this time, as humanity undergoes the collective shift in consciousness. Many blessings to you all.

Contents

List of Meditations and Exercises ... xi

Tips from the Subtle Body ... xiii

Disclaimer ... xv

Acknowledgments ... xvii

Introduction ... 1

Chapter One: An Introduction to the Subtle Body ... 13

Chapter Two: Subtle Body Awareness and Integration ... 51

Chapter Three: Why We Experience Dis-ease ... 67

Chapter Four: Healing Is Now ... 97

Chapter Five: Energy Medicine through Intention and
    Application ... 113

Chapter Six: Spontaneous Healing through Surrender ... 137

Chapter Seven: Unifying Mind, Body, and Soul ... 151

Chapter Eight: The Field of Healing and Miracles ... 165

Chapter Nine: Maintaining Inner Balance ... 189

Chapter Ten: Conscious Eating through Awareness ... 213

Chapter Eleven: A Paradigm Shift in Health ... 231

Conclusion ... 243

Glossary ... 245

Meditations and Exercises

Inner Being Meditation ... 21

Guided Wholeness Meditation ... 27

Feeling and Awareness Exercise ... 35

Inner Balancing / Neutralizing Fear Exercise ... 38

Subtle Body Awareness Meditation ... 54

Chakra-Activating Exercise ... 56

Clarity and Discernment Exercise ... 79

Transmuting Anger Exercise ... 90

Becoming Unstuck Exercise ... 100

Inner Peace Guided Chanting Meditation ... 106

Energy-Healing Guided Meditation ... 115

Cellular-Healing Guided Meditation ... 124

Chakra-Healing Exercise ... 128

Imagination Development Technique ... 132

Imagination Development Exercise ... 133

Oneness Chanting Guided Meditation ... 162

Self-Reflecting and Renewing Exercise ... 179

Trigger and Trauma Healing Exercise ... 195

Self-Love Chanting Meditation ... 200

Stress-Releasing Exercise ... 206

Tips from the Subtle Body

Five Tips to Cultivate Subtle Body Awareness ... 34

Ten Tips for Setting Healthy Boundaries ... 64

Five Spiritual Insights for Understanding
    and Dealing with Anger ... 89

Ten Mindfulness Tips for Inner Peace ... 105

Ten Timeless and Youthful Affirmations ... 111

Five Ways to Align with Living Inside-Out ... 146

Five Soul- and Spontaneity-Cultivating Tips ... 149

Ten Ways to Reconnect Mind, Body, and Soul ... 152

Five Ways to Activate Kundalini Energy ... 168

Five Awareness-Expanding 5D Reality Insights ... 182

Six Ways to Cultivate Mental and Emotional Stability ... 183

Ten Ways to Cultivate and Embrace Wholeness Daily ... 186

Ten Daily Inner Balance Reminders ... 190

Eight Ways to Practice Self-Love ... 198

Ten Self-Care/High-Vibrating Affirmations ... 210

Ten Ways to Practice Conscious Eating ... 217

Eight Tips to Cultivate Awareness ... 221

Five Ways to Align with the Subtle Body ... 225

Eight Tips for Nurturing the Body ... 227

Five Ways to Discover Your Passions and Purpose ... 236

Eight Insights Toward Spiritual Wellness ... 239

Disclaimer

This book's contents are for informational purposes only and are in no way a replacement for medical or mental health care. The information is provided for educational purposes and should not be relied upon as a substitute for a personal consultation with a qualified health care provider. Always seek the advice of a qualified health care provider if you have any questions regarding a medical or mental health condition.

Acknowledgments

A special thank you to my editor, Amy Glaser, who has the uncanny ability to ground me in my writing and bring me back to earth. She always offers a much-welcomed and needed perspective. You are always an absolute joy to work with. Thank you, Amy. To my production editor, Stephanie Finne, I can't thank you enough for your work on this project. Your clarity in assisting me on honing in on what I want to convey to the reader is so very much appreciated. Thank you very much, Stephanie. And to the rest of the staff and team at Llewellyn Worldwide, many thanks for all that you do.

Introduction

In this book, I introduce the profound restorative abilities of the energetic intermediary that connects the spiritual with the physical by sharing insights, awareness, and reflections on the healing nature of the subtle body. I will also provide tools and strategies (intentions, exercises, and meditations) to not only propel you forward on your healing journey but also assist you in creating the atmosphere for a potential spontaneous healing. It's my deepest desire that you remember that everything you need for health, wholeness, and healing is already within you. Healing is a process of letting go to allow for a renewed mind, a rejuvenated soul, and the physical healing that comes from wholeness.

A conscious reconnection with the subtle body and the chakras within it has the potential to heal and restore balance within us—mentally, spiritually, and physically. By being able to align with it and tune in to its infinite intelligence, the subtle body can guide you to greater harmony and peace as your vital energy and its flow is restored. The subtle body works as a messenger, imparting feeling and information, and when you can discern those messages, you can act on the cues that are telling you that you have come out of balance or alignment. With some understanding and clarity, you can integrate your awareness with the subtle body, get into more of a flow state, learn to shift back into balance, experience emotional relief, and develop tools to move forward rather than allowing negative emotions to keep you stuck. What all of this accomplishes is a healthier mind overall, which translates to greater health, beginning at the energetic level, because of the mind-body connection.

Working with the subtle body through awareness and following its divine guidance, you step into a more balanced, empowered, intuitive, and wholeness-centered state of being. When I say *balanced*, I mean in the sense that the automatic negativity we experience as human beings is counterbalanced by introducing positivity through spiritual integration and embodiment. We become more empowered as we become more spiritually aware, which includes becoming cognizant of our spiritual faculties and tools at our disposal, such as the releasing power of forgiveness and the reality-shifting potential of our intentions. Greater intuition is experienced as we tap into the discernment of spirit, allowing us to recognize the difference between inspiration and guidance versus fear. And by considering our spiritual nature, we are able to navigate life in a more holistic approach, as we become aware of the mind, body, and soul connection on a deeper level than ever before.

The subtle body is responsible for our automatic healing, as well as the flow of universal energy that emanates from the soul to our physical body through the chakras. When you are centered and in alignment in mind, body, and soul, you experience the natural flow of this energy (nonresistance, energetically speaking). In this centeredness, you allow for the restorative and healing properties of universal energy to fill your being with light, strength, and vitality. This is why reconnecting with the subtle body and embodying our spiritual nature is vital to experience healing, extraordinary health, and wholeness.

A Deeper Look at Wholeness

Let's start with a definition of *wholeness*, as it will not only provide clarity but also a clear goal that can be focused upon, resonated with, and aligned with so that it can be actualized and embodied. Wholeness is an awareness that has integrated one's spiritual nature to the equation of being human—it's the experience of being one in mind, body, and spirit. This is an empowering state to be in because being whole on a conscious level allows you to embody the attributes of spirit, such as clarity, understanding, peace, happiness, and strength, as you merge that expanded awareness with your humanity.

Health is known to be connected to one's vibrational frequency, which is the sum of one's outlook, thoughts, emotions, words, and actions. As such, being whole has profound, positive impacts on virtually every facet of one's life.

My focus throughout this book is on the awareness of the mind, the subtle body, and the soul, and their intimate connection with the physical body. It has been my experience that awareness truly is *everything*. That's because what we become aware of—as creative, spiritual beings—we give life to. Awareness takes potential and makes it a possibility.

I have also come to understand that when insights and wisdom come from higher dimensions of consciousness, they not only have inner energetic-shifting properties but reality-shifting power as well. What I mean by that is as we make shifts within ourselves and expand our awareness, we release life-robbing fears, old patterns, and habits, opening the door to a renewed mind, greater health and happiness, as well as new experiences.

As we move forward, I will offer the wisdom of the subtle body—the inner healer—and provide insights and clarity on topics such as the cause of dis-ease (which is an energetic state allowed to express physically) in chapter 3, how to create inner balance in chapter 5, and how to create the atmosphere for spontaneous healing in chapter 6. We'll also be looking at the roles the chakras, or energy wheels, play within the subtle body regarding health and well-being, as they have a consciousness of their own.

As you make breakthroughs and move beyond limiting ideas and beliefs regarding health and healing, you'll start the process of breaking down the walls of separation between your awareness and the soul. This will allow you to embody more of your spiritual, complete, and whole self. My wish is to remind you that your true, authentic, spiritual self is the key to not only healing dis-ease but also transcending it altogether.

Why Are We So Disconnected?

The vast majority of us have become so disconnected from the subtle body, and the soul for that matter, because of ego identification—solely identifying with the thinking mind. This causes our forgetfulness or lack of awareness. It's important to mention this, as there's no one to blame here, not even ourselves, because it's all part of the process of remembering who we are, spiritually speaking.

In forgetting who we are spiritually, we're able to have the full human experience, which includes the feeling of being disconnected from our spiritual nature and the subtle body. We all signed up for this spiritual amnesia because it's an adventure that the soul (you) decided to embark upon in order to experience being separated from the whole self and the challenges that come with it. This is chosen because in the spiritual realm a soul can conceptually know the idea of being cut off from itself, but it cannot experience it directly. Knowing that it cannot ever really be disconnected from its wholeness, the soul chooses to incarnate, take on an ego and physical body, and experience disconnection temporarily. In doing this, it sets itself up to experience the ups and downs of being human, including suffering, to create the desire to once again remember and return to itself—to wholeness. In the process of all of this, the soul learns what it's like being a human, and through this evolves and grows through various scenarios and experiences.

To clarify, it's not so much that we're disconnected, but rather we have forgotten. This is why awareness is key in this case—it opens the door to remembering and, in a sense, reconnects us consciously with our spiritual nature and all within it. In other words, awareness is like a wall-breaker, dissolving the imaginary wall of ego that separates us from the wholeness of our being: the soul.

How to Tell We're Disconnected

There are a few ways of knowing if we're cut off from our subtle body and spiritual nature. The subtle body communicates through feelings, our energy levels, and an overall sense of well-being, or lack thereof. Where our attention and focus go is also a good gauge for knowing if we're disconnected from our deeper aspects. The great thing about highlighting all of this is it gives one an idea of how much they are disconnected, which can potentially serve as the fire that lights the desire to shift inward and reconnect with spiritual aspects more deeply as well as the healing potentials within that expanded awareness.

Feelings

Let's start by looking at the idea of feelings as they relate to the subtle body. When we're disconnected from it and our spiritual nature, we experience the feeling of being separate from others, including the outer world. This is a direct result of feeling separate or disconnected from our inner being (the soul), which is connected with everything and everyone. As a result, we experience the feeling that we have to tackle life on our own, and that we're not being divinely guided.

Energy Levels

Being disconnected from the subtle body has one experiencing fluctuating energy levels and, more often than not, feelings of exhaustion. The subtle body is responsible for the flow of universal energy to us and through us, and when we operate through separateness (the idea of being separate from spirit) we bottleneck the flow of energy, limiting our vital energy. This can, and does, lead to energy imbalances, where some chakras allow more energy to flow while others allow less, depending on our level of awareness.

Sense of Well-Being

A diminished sense of well-being is another indicator of subtle body and spiritual disconnection. This is experienced as being overly reactive to others and the outside world, including circumstances, which impacts our levels of joy and happiness. When we're connected with our spiritual aspects, we feel a deep sense of well-being, even in the midst of adversity. However, that's not the case when we're disconnected.

Focus

Lastly, but probably most importantly, being primarily focused on the past and future with little to no awareness of the present moment is the best indicator of one's disconnection. When we're primarily operating between the past and the future, then we're more identified with ego and less with the soul. The ego creates that disconnection by having us focus outwardly, as it keeps us distracted with emotions from recognizing and remembering the stillness of our inner being.

My Journey to Spiritual Embodiment and Subtle Body Awareness

In the fall of 2005, after enduring several years of unease, worry, and a life-changing health scare, I awoke "in the twinkling of an eye" to the source of my suffering and the path to renew, restore, and strengthen myself in mind, body, and spirit. During those years of profound personal adversity, relief and the possibility of experiencing non-suffering were not only out of mind but seemed impossible. I was convinced that what I was experiencing was so real, so concrete, and a matter of fact, that living a life of peace, certainty, and vibrancy was only a dream. I was out of alignment in many ways. I didn't understand that I was manifesting my life, moment by moment, and that I was the cause to my effects, which included intense anxiety, the depression that came with it, and the cancer diagnosis I was given in 2004.

I've always been empathic, sensitive to my energies and the energies of those around me. By the time I'd reached the age of nineteen, the density of those energies began to have an impact on my life, including my relationships, health, and energy levels. Feeling that something was really off, I went the conventional route and saw my family doctor. He was caring and authentic, and he really wanted to help his patients to the best of his abilities. But here's the thing: physicians aren't trained in energy medicine, the power of awareness, and what it means to embody who we are spiritually or how to achieve wholeness in mind, body, and soul. I remember saying to my family doctor, "Doc, I have more courage in my pinkie finger than all my friends combined. I don't know why I'm feeling this way." His answer was, "It's anxiety." He wrote me a prescription and sent me on my way. After several months of side effects, yet finding no relief, I stopped taking the prescription.

Despite feeling continuously emotionally overwhelmed, I pressed on, year after year. I worked in my chosen profession as a dental hygienist and educator. Being caught up in linear time, the emotions grew, becoming heavier and more intense as time passed. The more I struggled internally, the more my relationships and life were impacted. I was feeling stuck and like every day was a repeat of the last. Little did I know that all the suffering I had been enduring all those years was setting me up for a spontaneous third eye activation—an awakening that changed the trajectory of my life in an instant.

Coming into early fall of 2005, I began dealing with even greater anxieties and worries than I'd ever experienced before: the fear of sickness and the fear of death following my cancer treatment. At times, the density of these emotions was incredibly heavy, almost unbearable. In November, I read a book by Dr. Daniel Amen called *Change Your Brain, Change Your Life*. On November 7, while sitting in my car during a break, I began to reflect on one of the phrases in the book. In the instant that I began to reflect, a voice—not a male or a female voice—came up through my chest and said audibly, "Challenge your thoughts!"

My forehead began to vibrate, and the negative thoughts and energies I had been enduring since I was nineteen began to automatically shut down. I remember turning my head and experiencing profound clarity. Believe it or not, I still had one patient left to work on before my shift ended. I went back to the office with this now-activated force and finished the necessary work on my last patient.

I got home after work, and this now-activated force between my eyebrows was still overwhelming. It was consuming the fear that I had been at the mercy of for so long. Feeling emotionally spent and coming into what I felt was a state of surrender, I jumped on the couch and said, "Just let me die." In that moment, I popped out of my chest. What I mean is that my awareness—my life force—left my body. At the time of this experience of "dying before you die," I didn't know where I went or how long I was gone. When I returned, I knew what had happened, and all the heaviness and years of emotional pain I had accumulated dissolved from my being in that moment.

Over the next thirty days or so, I went on to experience mystical events, profound insights, automatic writing, and a spontaneous healing. On a Saturday, I was meditating on my sister's couch when I suddenly experienced a vision of myself standing in front of "another me" in a wheelchair. The me that was standing placed a hand on the forehead of the wheelchair-bound me and my inner knowing was that I was healing myself. I then had a vision of a red brick wall with the word *ego* written on it. In the vision, I watched as this brick wall crumbled in my mind's eye. As all of this was taking place, a thought came to me, *Since I had healed my mind and my soul, my body is healed.* I immediately felt the joy of my soul bouncing up and down in the center of my body. In that moment, I was fully conscious of my soul. The tears that rolled down my face were so filled with gratitude, release, happiness, and joy that they left burn marks on my cheeks for three days.

In coming into the dimension of inner stillness, or soul awareness, I allowed clarity, insights, and the hidden mechanics of life to come to the forefront of my consciousness. I came to understand what wholeness is, how to embody it, and how to maintain inner balance, and I learned that power comes from surrender and letting go. I had tapped into the inner healer, and it revealed the secrets of the subtle body, its wisdom, and its guidance to heal: mind, body, and soul. By the end of November, I had my first speaking engagement on the healing potential of inner stillness and the power of consciousness through intention. By the end of December of that same year, I had written my first book, *Challenge Your Thoughts*.

After a few months passed, I decided to visit my family doctor to share the good news of my healing and give him a copy of my book. I explained that I experienced an awakening, became whole, and remembered to live in the present, moment by moment. Astonished at my news, but happy for me, he muttered, "Physician, heal thyself." My sense is that he'd never had a patient go through what I'd gone through and come out healed.

My Life Moving Forward

Every aspect of my life vastly improved once I reconnected with my spiritual nature and the divine guidance that comes from subtle body awareness. Being continuously connected to spirit and the subtle body provides the discernment to bring awareness to negativity as it arises, allowing it to be transmuted as it presents itself. I no longer suffer from anxiety and depression. Instead, I use any negativity that arises as a reminder to reawaken. This expanded awareness has resulted in the experience of operating from a high vibrational field, one where fear cannot last long.

With fear being put in its rightful place, clarity has been allowed to come front and center to my awareness. In that awareness, I am able to be divinely guided in all aspects of my life, including my overall well-being, relationships, and health. If I could sum up this state of awareness with one statement, it would be: I now live more in one breath than I ever did in the thirty-three years before my shift in consciousness.

Overcoming and transcending my personal adversities has allowed my soul purpose to unfold. In other words, I've realized that my suffering served a purpose, and it was to crack the shell of the ego so I could remember who I am spiritually. In my remembering, I can embody who I am, and in being so, I can remind others who they are. I can be of service.

How This Book Will Be Presented

My goal for this healing guide is to bring awareness to the potential of the subtle body and demonstrate what is possible when one is in alignment with its divine intelligence. I will be offering the clarity and wisdom of the subtle body through reflection, providing a spiritual perspective on the cause of dis-ease, its purpose, and how to invite and come into a space for healing.

Throughout this book, insights will be offered, along with exercises and meditations, with the intention to shift you energetically in a positive way, directing you inward, toward the wholeness of your inner being.

Why I Brought This Book to Life

I wrote this book for two main reasons. First, and most important, I realized there are some vital healing concepts and insights that are missing in this genre. Concepts such as what happens in the moment, energetically, to our chakras or energy centers when we operate through a reactive state and what we can do, in the moment, to bring instant balance and healing. Second, I have realized that there is a growing demand for understanding energy medicine and our innate ability to heal from within, as outer, conventional systems are revealing themselves to be outdated and ineffective.

In reading this book and applying its principles, you will become more aware of your ability to heal on the levels of mind, body, and soul, through the insights and the spiritual tools offered. You'll learn how to clear up stale, old energy; tap into the limitless reservoir of universal energy that is always available to us; and tune in to your inner healer (the subtle body), which is an extension of the soul. In becoming a master of your own energy and positive channeler of your life force, you will have the discernment and awareness, knowing when to shift internally to allow balance to unfold.

I have always found that reading a book from front to back initially and then going back to apply the exercises or meditations offers greater clarity and a fuller experience overall as concepts are applied. This book is also meant to be a reference guide and reminder—refer to it often. I have also discovered that when we return to a specific section of a book, we can receive greater insights and clarity the second or third time around. We receive the things we need, right when we're ready for them.

A thousand blessings as you embark on your healing journey to wholeness.

—Jiulio

Chapter One

An Introduction
to the Subtle Body

The subtle body is not entirely spiritual nor material; it is the intermediary between the soul and the physical body. Also described as the light body, the energetic body, and the astral body, this quasi-energy form is responsible for all of the physical body's functions, bringing it to life, in essence. The subtle body (an extension of the soul) is infinite intelligence encoded with all that is required to heal and maintain homeostasis, or inner balance on an energetic and physical level. When allowed to function without impedance—impedance being an imbalance of excess negative emotion—the subtle body expresses itself as vitality, strength, and extraordinary health.

The subtle body houses seven main chakras, or energy wheels, which are powerful energetic potentials that harness universal energy and express it as chi (life force). Starting at the base of the spine and moving up toward the crown, they are: the root chakra,

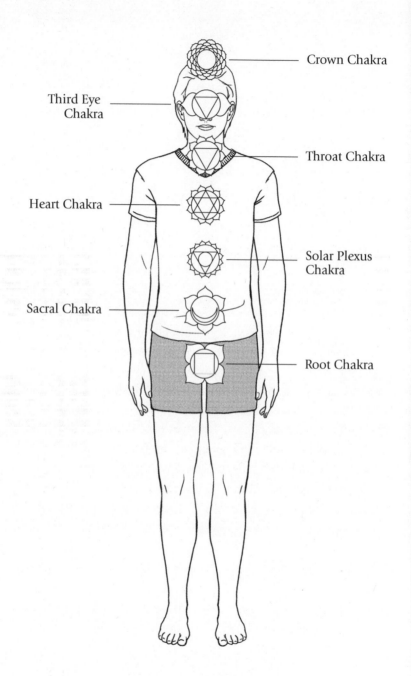

Crown Chakra

Third Eye Chakra

Throat Chakra

Heart Chakra

Solar Plexus Chakra

Sacral Chakra

Root Chakra

the sacral chakra, the solar plexus chakra, the heart chakra, the throat chakra, the third eye chakra, and the crown chakra. Each chakra is assigned to particular organs or regions within the physical body based on their location. Let's take a look at each chakra more closely, as to offer a greater overview of the subtle body's makeup and how it relates to the physical body.

The Root Chakra

The root chakra is located at the base of the spine, closest to the earth. When operating optimally, it expresses itself as stability and centeredness, and it gives you the feeling of being grounded. When this chakra is blocked by fear or uncertainty, you may feel insecure and unstable in your emotions.

The color associated with this chakra is red, as it represents our connection to the earth. As the foundation of the chakra system, a balanced and free-flowing root chakra is key in experiencing strength and overall mental steadiness. The organs and areas associated with the root chakra are the adrenal glands, colon, bones, and pelvic region.

The Sacral Chakra

The sacral chakra is located just below the navel. When unencumbered, the sacral chakra gives you the ability to be playful, sensual, and creative. Fear of judgment or reliving a past negative relationship negatively impact the energy flow of this chakra, and this may have you feeling detached and/or experiencing low self-esteem.

Orange is the color associated with this chakra, as it represents vitality. Because it governs your emotions and overall expression, being in touch with this chakra allows you to feel the lighter side to life and not take things too seriously. The reproductive organs, womb, bladder, and kidneys are associated with this chakra.

The Solar Plexus Chakra

The solar plexus chakra is located in the upper abdomen area. When in balance, it gives you a sense of self, personal power, and purpose. Lacking direction or feeling you're at the mercy of circumstances offsets this chakra, which may result in one feeling disempowered and indecisive.

The color yellow is associated with this chakra, as it represents your connection with the sun. Reflecting your willpower and confidence, being aligned with this chakra offers confident and assertive expression. Because of its location, the digestive system, liver, spleen, and gallbladder are associated with the solar plexus chakra.

The Heart Chakra

The heart chakra is the source for unconditional love, compassion, and forgiveness, and it is located in the center of the chest. Holding on to grudges, anger, and hatred creates a block in this energy wheel, resulting in feelings of self-loathing and a lack of empathy.

Green is associated with this chakra, as the color relates to charitable love. Being heart-centered is the wellspring for unconditional love and all that extends from it, allowing for deeper connections with others without the fear of getting hurt, as well as the ability to forgive. The heart, lungs, circulatory system, arms, and hands are associated with this chakra.

The Throat Chakra

In the center of the neck sits the throat chakra, which allows you to express yourself on an energetic and physical level. The fear of expressing yourself or being misunderstood closes the throat chakra, making it difficult to communicate your emotions and giving a sense of not being heard.

The color associated is blue, as it is connected with clarity. The central hub for self-expression and your ability to speak your truth, this chakra expresses as clear, direct, and honest communication. The mouth, tongue, pharynx, and neck are linked to this chakra.

The Third Eye Chakra

Found in the forehead between the eyebrows, the third eye chakra is the seat of clarity, wisdom, and intuition. It is the doorway to higher states of consciousness and enlightenment. Negative thinking and energy imbalances separate us from our inner guidance system, creating confusion and misunderstandings due to a lack of clarity.

Indigo is the color representing the third eye, or brow chakra, as it is associated with wisdom and the link between this world and the spiritual. The doorway to directly experiencing the highest self through inner stillness, the third eye elevates you beyond the thinking mind, offering the experience of oneness—of being one with everyone and everything. The pineal gland is associated with this chakra, as it serves as a receiver and transmitter of information.

The Crown Chakra

The crown chakra is located at the top of the head, and it connects you to your spirituality. It merges your conscious awareness to universal, or cosmic, consciousness—the mind of Source. Being materially focused and operating from the belief that you are separate from everyone and everything, including Source Energy, creates fears, anxieties, and a lack of clarity regarding the outer world.

Purple represents enlightenment and spirituality, and it is the color associated with the crown chakra. During the experience of expanded awareness, you're able to access latent spiritual faculties, psychic gifts, and higher dimensions of consciousness as you embody the spiritual self through an open crown chakra. Closely linked to the brain, the pituitary gland, and the pineal gland, these regions are associated with this chakra, as they are transformers for consciousness—translating higher dimensional information.

Physical Body Identification

Being completely or mostly physical body identified offers a different perspective and outlook from someone who sees themselves as a spiritual being first and foremost. Neither point of view is superior to another; it all depends on what is serving you wherever you are on your spiritual journey. By reflecting what the subtle body tells me, I'm going to shed some light on what happens as a result of identifying only as a body, rather than from the awareness of being a mind, body, and soul.

When one solely identifies with the thinking mind, the effect of that is to believe that one is a physical body and nothing more. That is because to the thinking mind, or ego, nothing else beyond it can exist. The idea of a soul, or even a higher mind, threatens its very existence. It's this uncompromising ego identification that closes one off to their spirituality and the reality of one's higher mind, which both reflect as inner stillness because the two—the soul and higher mind—are in fact one. Being both ethereal and reflections of one another, the higher mind and the soul are interconnected.

When one identifies as a physical body, that self-inflicted idea or sponsoring thought branches out, creating other limiting beliefs about oneself. A sponsoring thought is, in essence, a main or core belief that one has about themselves that then generates other thoughts, positive or negative. Our focus will be on the physical body and how a firm belief in it limits one in many ways.

Thinking that you're just a body convinces you that you're limited because it closes you off from the idea that you're actually a spiritual being able to call forth and even shift realities. This limited awareness leaves one feeling that they're at the mercy of luck or chance, their past, and their circumstances. You can see how the initial sponsoring thought can snowball and then branch out, creating more and more limiting ideas about oneself.

Physical body identification is a denser, heavier experience, energetically speaking, as it shuts the door to the light and the expansive experience of being aware of the soul and the higher mind. Reflecting the egoic (thinking) mind and its darker nature, the body accumulates negative energies, stores them, and allows for emotional pain to build. It's this negative energy—beliefs stored as information—that can override and thereby negatively impact the subtle body's intelligence and ability to maintain health and inner balance, causing dis-ease. Keep in mind that all of this is a process; one of forgetting who you are so you can experience what you're not in order to create the perfect storm of emotions, in a sense, to serve as a catalyst to awaken from the dreaming state of thought.

Seeing ourselves as just a body is what then paints others as just that. If you're just bodies, then you must be separate from each other, and you must be divided. It's what also veils one to the unifying spiritual world within, and that surrounds them. Heaven and hell are states of mind, and depending on your inner awareness, they determine whether you primarily experience oneness, joy, bliss, unconditional love, harmony, certainty or separation, fear, doubt, confusion, loneliness, and worry.

With all that being said, what exclusive physical body identification accomplishes is to subconsciously confirm the belief in sickness and the fear of death. If the physical body is real, then so too must be sickness and the thoughts that sponsor it.

In other words, either the physical body is real or the soul is. Either the egoic thinking mind with its ever-changing, dark nature is real or the soul with its unchanging, eternal essence that is stillness is. With regard to the idea of death: if the physical body dies, then so does the personality, the person themselves, according to the ego. Thankfully, spiritual awareness says otherwise. The physical body is mainly made up of space and, from a spiritual vantage point, is not who you are but what you, as a spiritual, eternal being, use to navigate the manifested world. Through that knowing, death is seen not as an end, or the end of one's existence, but as a doorway—a passage to experiencing more of the vastness of one's spiritual reality and all the unlimited aspects of it.

I now feel inspired to offer a meditation that focuses on and brings awareness to one's inner being, which can expand your awareness toward the subtle body. Shifting from strict physical body identification entails awareness of one's spiritual nature and higher mind. That is accomplished with reflection, mindfulness, and meditation. A spiritual teacher can point you inward and describe who you are beyond the thinking mind and body, but nothing truly can replace the direct experience of inner stillness—your inner being experienced as inner peace, clarity, wisdom, strength, and understanding through knowing, rather than belief. The following is a simple guided meditation with the intention to point you inward, beyond the physical body, and into the realms of your soul and higher mind.

⑤ Inner Being Meditation ⑤

To begin, place yourself in a comfortable meditation position. Sit up straight with head erect, or lie down if you wish. Drop your shoulders and shift into a state of just being present where you are. Your eyes can be open or closed. Follow your breaths for a few moments, as you become more relaxed.

Bring your awareness inward and just observe the thinking mind without judgment. In other words, first become aware of your thoughts. After a minute or two, bring your attention toward your own awareness, the "you" that is aware of thoughts. This is the silent witness, or conscious mind, that's experiencing the ego's thought process. This is the you that is silent (the inner being or soul) and is experienced as the nothingness, even as the gaps of space between thoughts. That nothingness is the very essence of your inner being; it is stillness. Bring your attention to the stillness and realize that is who you are, beyond the thinking mind and physical body. That is your core being and your eternal, indestructible, unchanging nature. Spend four or five minutes being aware of your inner presence.

Next, open your eyes, if they were closed. Through the space of stillness, look at your surroundings and notice that stillness extends, seeing always oneness. Allow that oneness—as nothingness, formlessness— to be reflected back to you. Be mindful that stillness is all-encompassing, found in everyone and everything. Continue with this for another four or five minutes of just being in the moment and aware of your very own awareness (stillness).

Once done with this meditation practice, take a deep breath and let go of the moment with gratitude. Allow the awareness of inner stillness to remain in your awareness as you feel comfortable.

This meditation of becoming aware of your spiritual nature can be practiced a few times a week initially, or practiced daily. As you become more aware of the presence of your inner being, the stillness of the soul, and your higher mind, the closer you will shift toward the complete embodiment of your spiritual self and the strength, oneness, and healing that emanates from it on a moment-by-moment basis.

Subtle Body Reflections

What I have realized on my spiritual journey and expansion of consciousness is that every part of our physical body—every system, organ, tissue, and cell, right down to every atom and beyond—has encoded within them intelligence, divine intelligence, in fact. This intelligence is based in consciousness, as everything in this reality springs forth from the All That Is.

Our oneness with Source Energy is a reality, as I have come to understand and directly experience through inner stillness. It's from this knowing that I have realized that every aspect to us (the mind, body, and soul, even our psychic abilities) have a consciousness of their own. In other words, every cell is aware and is listening to our thoughts, words, emotions, and outlook—all which make up our vibrational frequency, the field of energy from which we operate.

The subtle body is an extension of the soul and an aspect of consciousness; it is intelligence itself. Its role is to not only marry the spiritual and the physical—thereby making our physical experience possible—but also play the role of automatic healer and guide to assist us back to inner balance. It also works as a communicator—using feelings, or energetic signals—to guide us in making more conscious dietary choices, for example. In other words, its main function is to maintain life and the robust health that comes from being in alignment with its guidance.

I became aware of the subtle body and its reality as an extension of the soul shortly after my shift in consciousness. Through deep meditation, I have been able to feel its presence as a part of me, as waves of energy. I was immersed in a bath of unconditional love for several hours on the second night of my first three-day fast several years back and experienced its gratitude.

Primary Function

Also known as the light body, the subtle body's primary function is to connect your soul to the physical body. When I reflect on it and how it operates, I have come to understand that it's somewhat of a transformer, taking the incredibly high-vibrating energy that emanates from spirit and stepping it down, coalescing it, bringing life to the physical body, which allows one to have the experience of being human.

While we're on the topic of the human experience, the following needs to be emphasized: you *have* a physical body but you *are not* a physical body. To identify yourself as a physical body is to be steeped into the dreaming state, the thinking mind. There's nothing wrong with that, but sole physical body identification lowers your vibrational field by closing you off to your spiritual reality—having you believe you're powerless to the slings and arrows of the outside world—and convincing you that you're indeed separate from everything and everyone, including Source Energy. In reflecting on this information from the subtle body, it wants to remind us that it's not diminishing the experience of being human but relaying that there's more to us (much more in fact) that has been forgotten through spiritual amnesia.

Since spiritual amnesia has been mentioned, we should address "the elephant in the room" in a spiritual sense: one's spiritual reality. That is who you are and where you are, in fact. And we'll get to that discussion very soon.

Secondary Function

The subtle body's secondary function is that of healer, automatic healer, in fact. Being the infinite intelligence within every cell of your body, its role is to always bring the physical body back to health and maintain that health by offering its guidance as to what the body needs, nutritionally speaking. It's always offering you feelings about your food choices, and based on what you're deciding, determines the feeling it offers.

According to the subtle body, its guidance has gone unnoticed or ignored by many of us, which results in energetic imbalances that evolve into physical symptoms. As I've come to understand—and to be clear, no one is being punished here for their food choices—the physical body is speaking to you via feelings through the subtle body, part of your inner guidance system.

The subtle body offered me an example of how it uses feelings to guide us in our nutritional choices. Let's say you're deciding between a heavier, denser food, say a cheeseburger, versus something lighter, a chicken salad, perhaps. When you considered the heavier food, the subtle body offered a negative feeling about it—a quick energy signal expressing "not that" if it's not serving you at the time. When thinking about the lighter choice, you experience a more neutral or higher-vibrating feeling, essentially saying "go ahead." It's important to mention that the subtle body is not deciding what you eat, but rather its sole concern is the nutritional requirements the physical body calls for. There may, in fact, be times when it suggests the denser option because you expended a lot of energy exercising or it felt more calories are needed in that moment. It's all about balance. Unfortunately for the Western world, much of our food is overly processed, refined, modified, and stripped of its nutrition.

I was grateful for the example given and for the clarification received. I, for one, have disregarded the subtle body's guidance over food choices many times, as I'm sure many of us have. But I understand what it's trying to convey, and clarity tells me that what the physical body requires is different from what the ego—and one of its facets (gluttony)—craves.

The subtle body had insights to share on gluttony, revealing to me the following: Overindulgence (the consistent intake of excess calories) is a reflection of an energetic imbalance. We've all heard that phrase "too much of a good thing," and it holds true in this instance. Gluttony, like any other negative energy, is somewhat of a possessive entity, hijacking one's consciousness and always seeking to fulfill itself, but never really being satisfied.

Gluttony is sponsored by the ego (thinking mind) and, like other denser energies such as anger, hate, and jealousy, has negative impacts on you energetically, even impacting particular chakras, depending on the emotion. Thankfully, inner balance can be restored, ushering in healing, when conscious approaches and mindfulness are put into practice.

Third Function

Self-awareness, with regard to how one has been operating and the impacts of doing so, is key in healing. In other words, true healing and wholeness are all about facing the darkness with light, not bypassing it with ignorance. And so, this is the subtle body's third, but equally important, function: translator of higher spiritual concepts and ideas. It takes the soul's message, its inspiration, and relays it, as it relates to health on all levels of your being. It does this by using the third eye to impress images in your mind or your intuition (your inner guidance system) as feelings or instant knowings.

When I was searching for healing (which is wholeness in a sense), I wasn't aware what that entailed, but I somehow knew intuitively that for healing to take place, I would have to go to the root of it all. I would have to dig down deep and bring it all up to the surface for lasting change and healing to take place. I didn't have direction or a goal to steer me toward it; I just knew I was missing something.

Wholeness is the awareness of the oneness of mind, body, and soul. That awareness reflects as conscious choices, behaviors, and actions based on knowing who you are spiritually. Supported by living in the moment, being conscious of the eternal moment of now, you align with the current and flow of universal energy, allowing yourself to be continuously renewed on all three levels of being. Free of fear and the fear of sickness, your vibrational frequency, or field, is allowed to ever expand, allowing one to embody their next grandest version of themselves, together with their highest timeline.

⑥ Guided Wholeness Meditation ⑥

There are a few things to consider and to be aware of before we move into this meditation or any future meditations or exercises: What you envision or image yourself as is what is called forth instantly in the unseen, or spiritual realm. There is no time whatsoever there, only the eternal now. Know that what you see in your mind's eye shifts potential to possibility. Lastly, know that what you desire for your life is what Source desires for you. The Latin translation of the word *desire* is "of the father," meaning it's being inspired by the highest self, or Source Energy.

To begin, find a quiet space. Place yourself in a comfortable position, sitting up straight with your head erect or lying down is fine, just be relaxed. Let go of any tension in your shoulders, just drop them, and ease into the present moment. Follow your breaths for a few moments, allowing yourself to become more relaxed, yet present.

Now, with eyes preferably closed, bring your awareness to the third eye, the space between your eyebrows and about a half inch above them. Begin to imagine yourself standing on a grassy field. The sun is shining down on you, and the temperature is perfect.

Next, see yourself looking younger, stronger, and smiling, as golden light is being emitted from the center of your being, filling you entirely with high-frequency energy. You're happy, vital, and feeling energized, as you look at the field surrounding you. Repeat three times out loud with belief (please note that coming from an awareness of knowing is even more powerful), "I am one in mind, body, and soul. I am whole and complete." Spend three to four minutes envisioning this.

As you're imagining yourself in this empowered state, begin to feel the positive feelings as a result of that state. Feel the joy, gratitude, and happiness, as you envision yourself being that—*now*. Immerse yourself in these high-vibrating feelings for three to four minutes.

This part of the meditation is optional. If you wish, spend another two to three minutes seeing yourself doing things you used to do and want to again, feeling *now* what that would feel like.

When ready, take a few deep breaths and let the image go. Open your eyes and bring your awareness back to your surroundings. Give thanks that it's done—letting go of how and when it will come to pass.

This meditation can be practiced once or twice a week initially, and it only takes ten to twelve minutes to perform. As you become more comfortable with this practice, you can move up to once daily. It's important to be mindful to never insist on a particular outcome, as attachment is often a thief of one's inner peace, and the practice of letting go is what restores it. We often get caught up in linear time, and the sense of "waiting for something to happen," but that vibrational field places us in a continuous space of more waiting. In other words, you should let go and let Source lead.

Connecting, Receiving, and Working with Subtle Body Messages

The ultimate goal of working consciously with the subtle body is to raise your vibrational frequency, making the conscious return to wholeness that will renew your mind and re-energize your soul, allowing you to shift into a healthier, stronger version of you. A large part of any spiritual, or inner work, is awareness, as it leads to clarity. Clarity invites greater discernment, making it easier to discern when we're being led by the ego or guided by the soul. The key in discerning between the two is recognizing the difference in the density of energy that's being presented.

The ego, which we'll go into much more detail on in the next chapter, is lower vibrating and often attachment or fear based. Its messages are usually—energetically speaking—repetitive, heavier, and darker in nature. The soul, conversely, speaks as a soft, still voice, as inspiration or as high-vibrating feelings or nudges.

The soul will also use the subtle body to get a message across when something is not for you. You'll get a sense of "no" or a sick and/or twisted feeling in your stomach; that's your intuition speaking, asking to be heard and heeded.

Receiving Messages

According to the subtle body, many of us have forgotten how to read energy and how to receive messages from higher dimensions of consciousness. We're going to start by looking at how the subtle body communicates with us. Using feeling—subtle nudges at first—is how it initially tries to get our attention to tell us that we're shifting out of balance. Whether a person has just started smoking, began eating consistently in an unhealthy way, or has begun creating greater energetic imbalances through negative thinking or anxieties, the subtle body starts by sending discreet messages, such as "come back into alignment" or "don't, not a good idea," or a contracting feeling, at first. Left unnoticed or disregarded, the messages get louder over time, often manifesting as symptoms that inform you that something is off. This is nothing to be afraid of or react to, but this should be paid attention to and listened to, so that the correct actions—internally and externally—can be put into motion to return to balance.

The subtle body has also emphasized that the majority of us have become accustomed to fearing the body and its symptoms during the early stages of illness because of the disconnect between mind, body, and soul. According to the subtle body's wisdom, the physical body is nothing to be feared; it's a miraculous piece of organic machinery. When embraced as a gift and as an extension of your mental and spiritual aspects, it can accomplish wondrous feats and even experience spontaneous healing, given the chance.

Before we look at how to connect with the subtle body, let's briefly look at the roadblock that stands between us and connecting with it: our human conditioning. Human beings have identified themselves with the thinking mind and, as a result, the physical body as well. In doing so, we've opened ourselves up to experiencing and automatically believing the fears, doubts, uncertainties, and even confusion that comes from such identification. Not knowing who you are, spiritually speaking, and identifying with and recognizing mainly fear-based thoughts has translated that energy into emotions, or energy-in-motion, which negatively impacts our energy wheels (chakras).

What the subtle body points to is that most of us, if not all of us, have become distracted from hearing its subtle messages simply because of the ego's proximity to us and because it's a louder voice. However, we can make a shift and reclaim our inner power and vital energy in the process by revoking the ego's hold on our consciousness. This is done simply by choosing consciously what we believe in.

Giving the egoic mind your automatic belief perpetuates it in your consciousness—in your thinking mind. In other words, the ego needs your belief and consequent reaction to keep its grip on you. The moment you begin to really decide for yourself—ask yourself, "Is this an empowering thought?"—is the moment you'll have begun your personal journey to liberation (freedom from fear and the lower-density energies associated with it).

The subtle body goes on to say that as its messages go unheard, due to the spell that is the dreaming state of thought, the energies—the negative thinking that sponsored the behavior in the first place, be it smoking or overindulging in food—continue to accumulate. As these energies become denser and heavier, and as symptoms increase in numbers or severity, most of us become more fearful, thereby fueling the current negative energetic state. Over time, this accumulation of negative energy can, and often does, coalesce and manifest as dis-ease.

Dis-ease

The following should be mentioned, as to bring clarity to the topic of dis-ease: It doesn't have to be a permanent condition. In fact, from a higher dimension of awareness, dis-ease is seen as an energetic state that's being unconsciously chosen over and over again through fear by focusing on it, talking about it, and inaction.

Despite all that, resolution and relief is possible by realizing that it's an energetic state, by choosing differently, by shifting internally, and by taking the appropriate mind/body/soul actions. The truth of the matter is we're talking about energy in its various forms—as thoughts, emotions, even atoms and cells. It's all energy, and it has the potential to shift and change its polarity from negative to positive and even neutral states.

The subtle body is clarifying that over time, as its messages go unheard, negative energy accumulates, affecting not only one's mind but also the chakras, resulting in symptoms.

Polarity

Let's clarify a little more on the topic of polarity and how it pertains to human cells and health in general. Every cell has trillions of atoms, and within each atom are protons, neutrons, and electrons. The protons are positively charged, the neutrons have a neutral charge, and electrons are negatively charged. Let's take these three basic parts of the atom and relate them to one's mind, to one's self. You could say that the proton is similar to your conscious mind, positive in nature. The neutron, or center of the atom, is like the center of your being, still or neutral. The electron, being negative, represents the negative nature of the egoic, thinking mind.

When someone is overly negative or experiencing excess negative emotion, that creates an imbalance of energy that is felt throughout a human being. This can potentially spill onto other aspects of one's life. One could say they have an excess of negativity.

At the moment of one's awakening to their spiritual nature (as one returns to balance, to wholeness), the ego—the negative, shadow self—is cast out of one's consciousness due to an increase in vibrational frequency. The ego is now left orbiting one's mind; you're no longer attached to it, as it's no longer being identified with. You still experience the ego, but now you experience it through greater awareness—you're free, as you no longer identify with it because you've remembered your spiritual nature.

Let's look at this a little closer. The following description is a picture of what true inner balance looks like on an energetic level.

The proton (conscious/positive mind) is closer to the neutron, or center of one's being (stillness), while the electron (unconscious/ negative self) is farther away. Being centered in your neutrality (stillness) happens as you engage the positive, conscious mind with positive thinking, while also being aware of the negativity of the ego. You're observing it; no longer reacting to it, but rather using it as a reminder to re-awaken when it projects.

The darkness serves as contrast to your inner light. This is how the egoic, thinking mind should be utilized. One has to awaken to the darkness to see it for what it is, to perceive it differently, to have it shift from the source of one's suffering, to remember—it is a catalyst to awaken and re-awaken, as it's called for in the moment.

Upon contemplating this concept, I've come to realize that the inner and outer worlds are reflections: "As above, so below." Our inner atomic makeup is a reflection of our spiritual reality— spirit coalesced as matter. In other words, physical reality is actually spiritual in nature, when one remembers who they are beyond thought—beyond the ego. We are spiritual beings, and having temporarily forgotten the inner reality of spirit, we have also forgotten that the spiritual extends to the outer world; hence, all of life is spiritual in nature.

Connecting with the Subtle Body

Let's now look at how to connect with the subtle body, and how to become more open to its divine intelligence. It starts with awareness—with knowing the subtle body is a reality and that it connects the soul with your physicality.

The best way to connect with the subtle body is through feeling. This entails cultivating physical body awareness by placing one's attention inward. As you practice becoming more body aware, your awareness and subtle body connection will begin to deepen.

You will become more receptive to its messages, which often come through feeling.

Five Tips to Cultivate Subtle Body Awareness

I am providing five tips on how to cultivate subtle body awareness that will deepen your connection with it and make you more receptive to receiving its guidance and wisdom. These tips can be performed in any order on a daily basis.

- Take five minutes a day and sit in a quiet space as you contemplate that you are a mind, a body, and a soul. As you reflect, remember that the subtle body is that which connects your spiritual and physical aspects. When we place our focus on a concept, we invite that particular topic, that field of energy, to speak to us through images or inspiration.

- Be mindful that the present moment is where your spiritual nature is encountered. Within that space of awareness, we become more focused and receptive to divine guidance, including that of the subtle body. Being present is an inner awareness kind of action, which automatically shifts us closer to spirit and invites insights, making us more receptive to pick up on subtle body messages.

- Remember to lighten up and not take life too seriously. When we're overly focused on the outer world, all the drama and seriousness out there can distract us from our inner world of spirit, which is joyful and lighthearted.

- Another way to receive subtle body messages with greater clarity is to ask the subtle body to make its communication with you temporarily more pronounced as you learn to pick up on its cues, which include feeling and vibration. You can approach your request with something along the line of (you can think this or say it out loud), "I would like to become more aware of the subtle body and how it communicates with me. I am willing and open to receiving its divine guidance." The request needs only be asked once, then let go of how and when. This is a great foundation for understanding and being able to receive subtle body cues—when something agrees with the subtle body, the feeling is more neutral, even uplifting. When something doesn't resonate with it, even a food choice for example, the feeling will be more contractive.

• Feeling and having awareness of those feelings are the keys to being able to connect and receive messages from within. As awareness is brought to how we feel, there's a natural development that takes place.

⑥ Feeling and Awareness Exercise ⑥

I want to now offer two exercises that complement each other. I will start with the feeling and awareness exercise, as it sets the stage for becoming more aware of how your state of mind is reflected in the body so that you can be more in tune with both aspects and understand how they mirror each other. As you put this exercise into practice, it will assist you in developing a deeper connection to the subtle body, as your discernment on how to pick up its messages is honed in the process.

Set aside ten minutes for this exercise two to three times a week. As you become more comfortable looking within and more consciously aware of the mind-body connection, this practice of bringing presence and awareness to the subtle body and how you're feeling will become more automatic. Second nature, if you will. You're going to need a writing utensil and a pad of paper or an electronic device for this short activity.

Find a quiet space that is free of distractions. Become comfortable in a seated position. Take a few deep breaths, and just become present where you are.

You're going to start by bringing awareness to how and what you're feeling in the moment. Take the next minute or two to perform a body scan. Starting at the top of your head, moving down, feel the energies and sensations within and surrounding your physical body. Make a mental note of what you're feeling. Do you feel tense? Relaxed? Neutral?

Once the body scan is done, bring your attention and awareness to the thinking mind. Without judgment, observe the thoughts and emotions being presented to you for the next two to three minutes. Can you recognize any correlation between your current state of mind and what you're feeling in the body? Whatever it is that you're feeling, in mind and body, translate those feelings to words on your pad of paper or device. Spend two to three minutes making notes.

Once you've noted what you're feeling and experiencing, take a look at what has been expressed. Take a few minutes to reflect on the following question: Do you recognize the connection between what you're feeling in the body and what's going through your mind? Be mindful that there's no right or wrong answer here; this is an unfolding of awareness, and it's a process. The answer you give today could change next week.

Once you're done reflecting, save or discard what you've noted—what's most important is the exercise itself. Bring your awareness back to your surroundings, and if you feel inspired, give thanks for the awareness arising within you. As you train yourself to connect with the physical body—which is the doorway to the subtle body and the way it feels—you'll develop further awareness into the mind-body connection.

This exercise has brought awareness—your conscious mind—to the physical body and thinking mind. The conscious mind and the thinking mind are two different things. Your conscious mind is positive in nature, and it is an extension of your higher mind, based in the present moment. It is also silent in nature, as it is pure awareness that is free of thought. Your conscious mind is aware of your current surroundings as you go along your day.

The thinking mind is our human conditioning—the ego. It's negative in nature, operates between the past and the future, and is repetitive, never really wanting to recognize the present. By bringing awareness back to the physical body and thinking mind through this exercise, you will develop greater discernment and clarity, setting the foundation for greater subtle body connection and awareness overall.

⑥ Inner Balancing/Neutralizing Fear Exercise ⑨

Now that we've laid a foundation for cultivating feeling and subtle body awareness, let's shift our focus toward how to disarm fear and turn from a negative state to a neutral and even positive state. The goal of shifting into a more neutral, or thought-free state, is that it naturally raises your vibrational frequency, making you feel lighter, and offers profound clarity in your ability to discern between positivity, negativity, inspiration, fear, and subtle body messages. This exercise incorporates part of the last exercise, as awareness is further cultivated when moving forward. From the last exercise, we will bring awareness to the thinking mind.

This exercise is the inner action whereby you can, through conscious awareness, dismantle fear as you shift back into balance. As you begin to neutralize fear through observation, rather than reaction, you'll automatically begin the process of coming back into balance—hence the name of this exercise. Two goals are simultaneously being accomplished.

Through the human experience we've identified with the thinking mind (ego), we've come to accept as true—or believe automatically—virtually anything that comes to mind and, according to the ego, reject anything that threatens it. Allow me to clarify.

The ego, because of its nature, has the tendency to absorb experiences and convert them to thoughts, feelings, images, and emotions. There's nothing wrong with that; it simply is what it is and does what it does. What the ego also does, because of its fragility, is tend to discard or reject anything that contravenes its belief system, which threatens its very existence. This is why your conscious awareness—and discernment—is key in the healing process. These spiritual faculties give you a bird's-eye view, a clearer picture into how the ego has been operating, so that you can decide for yourself what is true or no longer true for you. In other words, belief creates personal reality, and our beliefs are what shape our experiences, including our health.

The return to wholeness is the remembering of who we are in a spiritual sense. It is the realization that nothing has to be added to us, but rather, we are to release that which has divided us from our completeness and wholeness. The divider in this case is the egoic, thinking mind, which has convinced us that we're separate in mind, body, and soul. Healing begins at the level of the mind, which is inspired by the soul, and will be experienced tangibly through the physical body—hence the journey back to wholeness.

To begin the exercise, find a quiet space that is free of distractions. Become comfortable, sitting or lying down. Take a few deep breaths and just become present where you are.

Bring your attention and awareness to the thinking mind. Without judgment, observe the thoughts, feelings, and emotions being presented to you. Begin to discern what is appearing negative or positive in terms of thoughts or emotions. Negative thoughts are fear-based, denser, separating, and contracting. Positive thoughts are love-based, lighter, unifying, and expanding.

If you find that a thought is negative—fear, anger, worry, or anxiety-based, and disempowering—*realize that you have a choice*. You can choose to automatically believe the thought, based on past data, thereby reacting and perpetuating the cycle of fear, or you can starve it of your vital energy by choosing to observe it, by giving it no belief whatsoever, and letting it go.

If you've decided to observe the negative thought or emotion through nonreaction, which neutralizes it, you can then take the next step: challenging the negative thought with a positive, life-affirming thought. For example, if a fear-based thought arises as "I'm stuck" or "I'm never getting ahead," you can replace that thought with a present-based and desirable choice of "I am already moving forward" or "I am unstuck now." In other words, take whatever fear or negativity is being presented and meet it with a positive, conscious thought. When you affirm the positive thought, do it with belief and conviction; better yet, with knowing.

Once you've replaced the negative thought with a positive one, the last step is to remember. Be mindful of the present moment. Bring your awareness to the here and now. In other words, remind yourself to get out of the repetitive, energy-draining cycle of past and future, and allow yourself to be renewed in mind through the now.

This exercise should take five to ten minutes initially. As you develop more awareness and cultivate this practice, you may find yourself practicing this self-empowerment strategy throughout the day.

To recap, you're bringing *awareness* to the thinking mind as you apply *discernment* to the thought, deciding if it's empowering or not. This leads you to the choice to give it *belief* or *not*, and then from that space, *challenge* the thought if it's fear or negative, as you remember the *present moment*. These are the keys and the formula to transmuting negativity as you raise your vibrational frequency.

A Few Notes on Ego

There are a few more things to be cognizant of. First, the ego can only offer you what it is: the darkness to our light. It operates by reliving the past and projecting it into the future, thereby perpetuating itself and its denser energies. The more clarity you bring to it, the more space, relief, and upliftment you'll begin to experience, as well as a renewed sense of well-being.

Next, the ego, being the source of our suffering, has no real rhyme or reason for presenting to us what it does. However, from a spiritual vantage point, clarity tells us that it serves as a catalyst for awakening: we take suffering and use it to create the desire for nonsuffering and the healing that comes with it.

What should also be mentioned is that as you observe and starve fear through nonreaction, you burn it up through the power of your inner light (consciousness). In other words, you're not suppressing or keeping anything in, but rather dissolving and alchemizing that which no longer serves you. Your inner being, the soul, is more than capable of transmuting any negative energy, as it is unconditional love, in essence.

It's also important to remember that you have time to choose differently. We are in a reality that has the experience of space and time. Just because a fear has been presented to you doesn't mean it's done and will manifest. You have time, in the moment, to observe rather than react and to consciously choose a more positive, life-affirming thought. I felt this was vital to mention because, for many, the natural instinct is to panic when negativity arises. I want to remind you that you can be calm in the knowing that you can choose another thought and a different, more desired, timeline.

The exercise of observing, challenging, and replacing negative thinking with positive thoughts can begin with a frequency of once or twice a week, if you've never done it before, eventually making it a daily exercise. The potential is there for you to come into such a space of clarity and awareness that you'll be able to neutralize fear and negativity on a moment-by-moment basis. Desire is the key in wanting to make lasting inner change, and "practice makes perfect," as it hones your spiritual faculties of awareness and discernment.

Invulnerability: A State of Mind

Invulnerability is an attribute of the soul—its strength—as it reflects its oneness with Source Energy. To become aware that such a state exists makes that potential within you a possibility. Your soul is invulnerable. It emanates and is the pure expression of unconditional love and the unimaginable power and unrestricted energy that flows from its connection, its oneness with the All That Is, or Source.

The soul is indestructible, eternal, multidimensional, and limitless in every way. It is pure potential and a force that, to be honest, is beyond words and comprehension. Invulnerability can start off being a concept, but it can absolutely become a tangible experience when you are one in mind, body, and soul. That is accomplished and directly experienced when one is deeply anchored in the present moment and experiences the inner stillness of the soul, which allows high vibrational, cosmic energy to flow through the mind and body, making them resonate with spirit, or Source Energy.

I want to start with the following as a foundation, to reveal how you can shift your awareness toward invulnerability, allowing it to show up in your life consciously. When you cultivate the practice of letting go of limiting thoughts and ideas regarding health and open your mind to expanded spiritual health concepts, you begin to resonate less with the conditioned mind and more with spirit. When you shift your awareness inward, contemplate what it means to be a soul, and align your awareness with stillness through the present, you become receptive to spiritual insights, which include what health is to the soul itself.

To the soul, sickness or lack of any kind doesn't exist, as its awareness is one with Source Energy. Unchanged and unmoved by being with the physical body or this world, for that matter, the soul is sovereign, despite having the temporary experience of being human with its limitations. The invulnerable state is, as I've come to know and experience, the embodiment of one's spiritual nature—the awareness that one is not their thoughts but the soul, the pure awareness—experiencing them.

It's the clarity, wisdom, understanding, and flow of power that arises when limiting ideas about health, relationships, abundance, and who and where you are, are laid aside and replaced with the inner knowing of the spirit. In the invulnerable state, as I experience it, the thinking mind is quieted by the awareness and presence of inner stillness (the soul itself). The inner light of consciousness is allowed to rise to the forefront of one's mind and the entire being is filled with light. That light contains information in the form of extraordinary health, spiritual awareness, and knowing.

The invulnerable state shifts you from operating from the outside-in to the inside-out. Allow me to clarify. Human conditioning has taught people to focus on the outer world. Because of that, the outer world is a very concrete reality in their minds, very matter of fact, as it's repeated in one's consciousness. This mode of operation causes reaction to take place while convincing one that the source of their suffering is "out there." If that's the case, then one must be a victim to their circumstances and to the forces beyond them. That is a disempowering state to be in, as it makes one vulnerable to the slings and arrows of fear. In essence, an invulnerable state of mind makes one unharmable—to the negativity and reactive state of the ego, and its fears. It's quite an empowering state to embody.

Operating from the inside-out is a conscious choice, one where the outside world is observed rather than judged because the understanding is that the outer is an extension of one's consciousness—that they are in fact one. To judge the outer world, to limit it with negative thought, is to only limit and attack oneself, energetically speaking. By realizing that the outer world is a reflection of one's inner world is to see the outer as not so much physical in nature but spiritual.

When you awaken to the fact that you're a spiritual being having a human experience, you begin to understand that physical matter—all of it, not just the physical body—is spiritual energy, or "universal mind stuff" coalesced. If one were to look at anything closely enough, one would see that space is what makes up the majority of any manifested material, biologic or otherwise. In becoming aware of and embodying your spiritual nature, by being the silent witness (who you really are), you become one with the highest self, also reflecting its attributes, which include invulnerability. In essence, one becomes unharmable in the invulnerable state, unmoved by the outer as one is centered in the strength of stillness from within.

Now that the concept of invulnerability has been highlighted, let's look at some ways it may have shown up, and can show up, in your life. You tap into the invulnerable state whenever you chose peace over conflict. It can show up in your life as a feeling of renewed strength or vitality when you're deeply anchored in the present moment. Invulnerability is strength. When forgiveness is extended to another, we are expressing strength through unconditional love, which is the foundation for invulnerability itself. It especially can show up in your life as a feeling of being centered in those moments where you feel one in mind, body, and soul.

You can cultivate and work through developing the concept of invulnerability to have it become a very tangible experience. Everything always starts with awareness; becoming deeply aware that you are a soul having a human experience is where to start. This can be revealed to you directly through inner stillness as you practice meditation.

Understanding that invulnerability is a spiritual attribute reminds you that it's not something that has to be added to you but what you need to become aware of. Living from the inside-out, rather than our conditioned way of outside-in, is one of the most powerful and transformative things you can develop in terms of becoming unharmable or invulnerable. In other words, the art of observing, rather than reacting to the outer world, is key.

I would be remiss if I didn't mention these last two positive forces: faith and trust, which have the potential to neutralize fear, the roadblock to invulnerability. Cultivating faith and trust can assist you in shifting from belief to inner knowing. And that's the goal with the concept of invulnerability: to know that you are invulnerable because that's what the soul is.

Three Keys to Health

We're going to take a mind, body, and soul approach toward health. Let's look at ways to invite greater health and wholeness back into your life through awareness, cultivation, and embodiment. For health to be experienced, tangibly, we need to acknowledge and address every aspect to us. To ignore a particular part of ourselves is to experience disharmony or imbalance in that particular aspect. We're going to start with the mind.

Mind

Awareness: The mind is the doorway to greater health. When illuminated, it is reflected as physical health. Being aware that health—good or bad—is an energetic state that becomes translated physically based on our thoughts, words, emotions, and outlook is key to understanding how we can take steps internally toward wholeness. As thoughts change, we shift into different states, and we experience this throughout the day. If the goal is to change a state that's been chronic, we have to change what thoughts we're thinking and what we're focusing on. The term *chronic* is relative, when looking at it from a spiritual perspective. When we identify with linear time—a past, a present, and a future—we experience time as if it were stretched out months and years, and we identify with thoughts similar to "it's been a long time." But to come from a space of awareness that the present moment (the eternal now) is all there ever is, one transcends linear time, and then words such as *chronic* become a thing of the past. Taking time to reflect on the concepts of past, present, and future moments can be awareness building.

Cultivation: We are either moving toward greater health or moving away from it. The mind is a powerful tool, and because of that, it requires direction. Leaving the mind to the uncertainty, doubt, fear, and confusion that comes from the ego leaves little room for wholeness. One must apply awareness—awareness of the present moment—not just daily but on a moment-by-moment basis to uproot "future" fears, fears of sickness and dis-ease, in order to bring energetic balance back. Setting a vision, a goal for great health or for any other facet of your life, is what shifts you forward, getting you unstuck and moving forward. Meditation, reading, or listening to inspirational material are great ways to cultivate the mind.

Embodiment: Bringing awareness to the thinking mind and realizing what it is, relative to your spiritual nature, affords you the ability to align with your true self and true conscious mind and its positive aspects. The positive mind takes goals and puts them into action through planning, vision, and choosing to become the version of yourself that you desire to experience, now, not in some future moment. In other words, as you plan, start to think, speak, and express who you desire to become, starting today. Setting a goal, writing out a plan, and starting to execute it are ways to embody what you're envisioning for yourself.

Body

Awareness: Being aware of the mind-body-soul connection and how the physical is a reflection of one's inner world puts you in greater sync with the body. This creates greater body awareness and the ability to discern the body's signals, shifting your awareness closer toward your intuition and inner guidance system. As you become clearer through awareness, you become more adept at paying attention to the physical body's needs versus what the egoic mind craves, for example. Practicing yoga and spending a few minutes from time to time just scanning the body from head to toe with your attention are ways to enhance body awareness.

Cultivation: To cultivate physical wellness and strength, the body needs to move regularly. Twenty to thirty minutes of physical activity, such as walking or strength training, can have tremendous benefits. Getting enough sunlight, rest, and proper hydration are also key in maintaining health. Positive thinking—having a loving and grateful attitude toward the body—is also incredibly important in developing a healthy relationship with it.

Embodiment: Taking a mindful and spiritual approach toward the body gives you the tools to make conscious decisions. Choosing to primarily eat a balanced diet, one that is full of nutritious food, will serve to fuel the body and give it the requirements it needs to function optimally. Managing stress consciously through self-awareness, getting physical activity, taking a few minutes a day for deep breathing, and creating a healthy body image through self-love and acceptance will greatly serve you in your healing journey.

Soul

Awareness: You can't experience wholeness without the oneness of the soul. Becoming aware that the soul (your authentic, true self) is already whole and complete is a huge part of the healing process. Being soul-aware gives you the clarity and discernment to not only know when to address fear or negativity but also the intuition to assist you in listening to your physical body's innate wisdom. Your source for inspiration (the soul) works together with the subtle body to be your guides, reminding you of what's possible. Spending time in silence or outdoors are wonderful ways to reconnect with the stillness of the soul.

Cultivation: Remembering the various attributes of the soul—compassion, kindness, forgiveness, joy, bliss, and wisdom—brings these gifts to life and to the forefront of your mind. As you remember these spiritual qualities, you open yourself to more divine inspiration and pearls of wisdom through the spirit of remembering and allowing. Focusing upon your divine nature shifts you closer to center and the unconditional love that emanates from your being. Practicing self-understanding by examining your beliefs and cultivating forgiveness are powerful ways to develop and grow spiritually.

Embodiment: Choosing love over fear is how one begins to embody their spiritual self. In other words, you must become that which you desire to experience. Speaking your highest truths, being authentic, and aligning consciously with the peace of inner stillness through present-moment awareness allows for the soul to express in your doingness. Remembering to practice the art of nonattachment, which is observing the ego rather than identifying with it, is a way to be spiritually mindful, which will point you inward toward the wholeness of Self.

Chapter Two
Subtle Body Awareness and Integration

The subtle body communicates through feeling, vibration, and intuitive "hits" by sending instant messages—downloads, if you will—to get its message across. It will also use thought in a subtle way. When those cues are missed or ignored, the messages grow louder, becoming experiences such as emotions or symptoms.

Working with the soul, the subtle body takes energetic information, wisdom, and guidance, and translates it. For example, when there's an energetic imbalance regarding a relationship that's experienced as conflict and disharmony, we feel it within us. An imbalance in the way we see and approach money leads to emotional experiences of lack and "not enoughness." An imbalance in our relationship with food and eating translates to body messages such as upset stomach, bloating, or a general disagreement with what's being consumed. The focus here will be on listening to the body's cues—when it disagrees with something or not.

The physical body's wisdom is always in communication with us, providing feedback by the way we feel. Our awareness of our spiritual connection, or the degree of the depth of that connection, determines how open and able we are to pick up on those feedback messages. Like any other imbalance one experiences in life, whether in relationships or in health, life will provide feedback in the form of emotions and in the way one feels.

The focus here will be on health as it relates to nutrition. When food is not in alignment with what the physical body needs, feedback is provided. It's provided not just after being consumed but also beforehand and even during the process. The subtle cues (e.g., a contracting feeling of "no, that's not what the body wants right now") often go unheard, mainly because there's not enough intensity behind them. Left unchecked, the subtle cues begin to manifest as symptoms—an irritable stomach, a feeling of heaviness, and tiredness after a large meal or after having consumed too much sugar. This is the subtle body speaking to you through the density of the physical body, telling you a change is needed and it's time to come back to balance.

Ignored year after year, the emotional issues (or negative feelings) that sponsor one's eating habits can then, combined with the poor nutritional choices, begin to manifest as dis-ease, such as diabetes, obesity, as well as other conditions. However, no condition is permanent, from the subtle body's point of view, if there is a conscious change in vibration and a change in diet. It should also be noted that when food that is in alignment with the body's needs is consumed, the experience is one of neutrality and even upliftment. A sense of calm is experienced, in other words.

Changing Your Vibration

As I reflect on the concept of changing one's vibration, I've realized there's been no real discussion on changing one's inner state, together with their diet, to shift back to health and to wholeness. From one point of view, Western medicine has fallen short in its approach to health and healing in terms of preventing and reversing dis-ease.

Focusing on the dis-ease, and not what causes it in the first place, is what perpetuates the unconscious approach to health. Upset stomach? Here, take this over-the-counter/prescription pill. All while there's no discussion that what one is consuming emotionally and nutritionally is what is actually causing the symptoms and eventual dis-ease. And there lies the snare.

Don't get me wrong, medicine certainly has its place, especially in the case of emergencies and when life-saving surgery is needed. But it falls short in its potential to integrate mindfulness with science—the spiritual science of the body. What I would also add, as more people awaken to their spiritual nature, is that true health and the concept of wholeness is being placed squarely in the hands of the individual because I don't see the establishment changing anytime soon.

Over the past few years, I think most of us would agree that we've been witnessing the struggle, and even collapse, of different systems, such as financial and healthcare. On a collective level, we're all realizing they're not working any longer. By becoming proactive and more self-responsible toward our health through the cultivation of awareness, mindfulness, and improving one's diet (choosing lighter, higher-vibrating foods, preferably non-gmo and organic more often), one can embody greater health and vitality with less reliance on outer systems.

As humanity continues to awaken during this time of great change on Earth, we're all being called to step into our sovereignty more fully. It won't be a stretch to apply that self-responsibility to the mind-body connection, which includes health.

⑥ Subtle Body Awareness Meditation ⑨

I want to now offer a short, simple meditation that will assist you in becoming more aware of the subtle body. When one becomes aware of the energy within and surrounding the physical body through the present moment, the subtle body can actually be felt and experienced as gentle waves of energy. These waves can be felt in the face and throughout the body.

Find a quiet space and get in a comfortable position. You can be sitting up or lying down for this meditation. If you're sitting up, drop your shoulders, relax, and let go. Eyes can be open or closed. Take a few slow breaths and bring your awareness to the here and now. Just become present in the moment you're in.

Now bring your awareness to the physical body, beginning with your face and head. Spend three to four minutes just being aware of these areas. Also become aware of the energy within and surrounding them. Just observe, if your eyes are open, and feel.

Then shift your awareness to your torso. Become aware of and feel the energy within and surrounding your torso. Again, just observe and feel. Practice this for three to four minutes.

Finally, repeat the process with your arms and legs. Feel the energy within and surrounding them. Just observe and feel. Do this also for three to four minutes.

Once you're done with these areas of the body, take three deep breaths and let the moment go. Bring your awareness back to yourself and your surroundings. Give gratitude for the experience if you feel inspired to do so.

A lot can be accomplished with this meditation in a short amount of time. This meditation needs only to be practiced once or twice a week, and it should take no longer than fifteen minutes.

Awareness is everything, and as you become more aware of the subtle body through desire and willingness, you'll open the door to experiencing it more tangibly, along with its wisdom and inner guidance. I should also note that the subtle body could very well be a doorway to reconnecting consciously with the soul. Becoming one with it in mind and body will allow you to embody the strength and vitality of wholeness.

Chakra Activation

The chakras, being housed within the subtle body, play an integral part in our emotional stability, energetic health, and overall sense of well-being. Bringing one's attention and awareness to these powerful energy converters brings life to them, as they are energized in our minds. The mind is that which generates reality, and what we see and imagine within our psyche and hold as true is called forth and experienced, sooner or later. Intention is everything when it comes to energy and manifestation, as it directs unseen universal forces to work on our behalf.

The benefits of activating and working with the chakras are many. Chakra work assists in bringing our energy back into balance. It opens the door to greater self-understanding, as we are much more than meets the eye. Having activated and optimal-functioning chakras grounds us in our spirituality, providing us with great strength and mental stability. In the face of stress or negativity, having a foundation of centeredness through subtle body and chakra awareness acts as a guidance system, pointing us back to center when we're temporarily thrown off-kilter.

The key to chakra activation is connecting with them through awareness, intention, and merging our imagination with them. They are powerful potentials within us, and we shift closer to higher dimensions of consciousness and an expanded version of ourselves as we realize their reality within us. That is because the chakras are doorways that connect this reality to the quantum world: the realm of spirit. Merging our awareness with these spiritual faculties deepens our connection with our spirituality, and the gifts found within expanded consciousness, which include psychic abilities and wisdom.

⑥ Chakra-Activating Exercise ⑥

I'd like to now offer a chakra-activating exercise based on the subtle body's suggestion. This light-activating exercise will shift you closer toward spiritual and subtle body awareness, allowing more light into your heart and mind. This exercise can be practiced weekly, and it should only take eight to ten minutes.

For this exercise, find a quiet area that's free of distractions. It is best if you are sitting up, back straight, and head erect. Close your eyes, drop your shoulders, and take a minute or so to breath deeply, as you become present, aware, and relaxed.

As you come into a more relaxed state, imagine seeing yourself as a light-body—a body filled with golden light. You are virtually entirely energy in this visualization. As you imagine this, picture the seven chakras with their colors. Starting from the base of the spine, moving up, swirling, and spinning in a clockwise fashion—at a perfect pace.

As a reminder: the root chakra is red, above it the sacral is orange, above that the solar plexus is yellow, above that the heart is green, above that the throat is blue, above that the third eye is indigo [a color between blue and violet], and at the top of the head the crown chakra is purple. Imagine this in your mind for two to three minutes.

Next, you're going to imagine the environment all around you and the energy within you raising and energizing, becoming more light filled. Now because you're one with your environment, you merge with it, allowing that energy to flow freely and fully into every chakra—all at once or one at a time, if it's easier to imagine. Imagine this for the next three to four minutes. As you imagine this powerful activation, drop your shoulders again, further surrendering and relaxing into the moment.

Once you're done imagining, take a few deep breaths, let the image go, open your eyes, and come back to your surroundings. Take a few more breaths, and give thanks for the moment and for chakra activation.

Two Voices: Love and Fear

Clarity reveals that essentially there are only two ways in which to operate from: love or fear. Of course, one can operate somewhere between these seeming opposites, but from an elevated point of view, light and dark are the choices we have. Be mindful that we are never judged from the space of awareness from which we operate from; however, we do immediately experience the fears we project and the love that we extend as feelings. Projection is what the ego does: painting another person or its own host and the world it experiences through its darker, separating, and limiting point of view. Extension is what emanates from the soul, as it shares what it is in essence: unconditional love, which is light-filled, inclusive, unifying, and expansive. Being able to become aware of how the ego and the soul communicate is key in cultivating greater discernment between the dark and the light.

The ego is fear, in and of itself. It communicates through past experience, which from its point of view limits present-moment reality, attempting to achieve its goal of diminishing the now moment. It also takes past experience and projects it as the future, so that it can not only perpetuate itself but limit your potential and possibility through fear and the contraction of your vibrational field. The ego at its core is fear, but it comes disguised as a variety of negative emotions and feelings, such as shame, anger, guilt, worry, anxiety, disgust, hate, frustration, boredom, loneliness, jealousy, resentment, and feelings of sadness, aggression, self-loathing, a lack of interest in life, and a lack of self-love. Through these lower-vibrating energies, the ego, when believed in and given our vital energy through reaction, becomes a reality. When allowed to hijack our consciousness through these energies, one will think, speak, and act upon these frequencies from an awareness of separation from the soul.

Conversely, the soul is unconditional love. It inspires and communicates always through the high-vibrating field of the present moment, where it offers insights, guidance, and flashes of genius. The soul expresses not emotion but its very self as divine experiences of bliss, joy, peace, clarity, wisdom, understanding, authentic happiness, compassion, wholeness, kindness, forgiveness, spontaneity, self-appreciation, and love without attachments or conditions. Being in soul alignment through awareness, one becomes the embodiment of who they are spiritually. They can then communicate and take action in an empowered and more conscious way, through the awareness of oneness.

The point here is not to judge either mode of operation but rather to offer clarification through insight into the shadow self (conditioned mind) and the soul (inner being). With clarity we can become aware of the dark and the light, allowing us to become more fearless through understanding and more conscious in how we operate, see ourselves, and see the world around us. Knowing how each aspect presents itself gives one the ability to discern through greater self-awareness.

Words Matter: The Power of I Am

In this section, we'll focus on life- and health-affirming words and phrases that are not only in alignment with the subtle body but also are inspired from the highest self. Before I offer a list of these words/phrases, let's have a look at the powerful, commanding phrase that sets off universal forces: I Am.

Using the phrase "I Am" activates the power of Source Energy, as one aligns their desire by choosing to become it now, not sometime in the future. By using the present tense, we energetically become one with the desire. The key, during this process of conscious choosing, is to let go of how and when the desire will manifest and what it will appear as. Attachment is a thief; one that steals our inner peace through conditions and frustration when we get caught up in linear time and base our happiness on the outcome, forgetting to enjoy the process. In other words, happiness, joy, bliss, even fulfillment are available now, through soul awareness—the direct experience of Source through inner stillness.

Here's a list of twenty-one general life-affirming, soul-inspired affirmations and the negative feelings they counteract. You can choose to align with, think, and speak as you feel called to. These affirmations are not based in the past but instead in the potential and possibility that comes from soul alignment. If a particular affirmation doesn't resonate right now, choose one that feels in alignment with you. You can always come back, re-evaluate, and choose again. The key is to really feel what you're expressing as true, as a known fact. You want to shift from believing in what you're stating to knowing it's true, and that it's done with conviction. You can think/speak these phrases throughout the day to counteract negative thoughts/feelings. As they build momentum through repetition, you may find (through the power of awareness you're giving them) that other life-affirming and conscious thoughts may come to mind.

Life-Affirming Phrases

- **I am whole and complete.** Counteracts feeling less than

- **I am fearless.** Counteracts feelings of fear

- **I am always divinely guided.** Affirms your divine connection to your spirit guides

- **I am beyond perfect health.** Counteracts thoughts of sickness

- **I am inner peace.** Counteracts feelings of uneasiness
- **I am safe and secure.** Counteracts thoughts of feeling unsafe
- **I am finding that everything works out for me.** Counteracts the idea that nothing ever works out
- **I am happiness.** Counteracts feelings of sadness
- **I am already healed.** Counteracts the feeling that healing is impossible
- **I am joy.** Counteracts feelings of misery
- **I am strength.** Counteracts thoughts of weakness
- **I am bliss.** Counteracts feelings of sorrow
- **I am renewed in mind, body, and soul.** Counteracts feelings of heaviness
- **I am unlimited.** Counteracts feelings of limitedness
- **I am free of the past.** Counteracts the feeling that the past is haunting you
- **I am abundant and prosperous.** Counteracts thoughts of lack
- **I am one with Source.** Affirms your oneness while counteracting feelings of loneliness
- **I am clarity and understanding.** Counteracts feelings of confusion
- **I am moving forward.** Counteracts feelings of being stuck
- **I am younger and stronger every day.** Counteracts age-related thoughts
- **I am unconditional love.** Affirms your true essence while counteracting feelings of hate

Self-Awareness Is a Superpower

I'll be going in-depth on the dimension of inner stillness and its potential and power to heal in chapter 8. However, I feel it is important to offer a glimpse into stillness and introduce it here as a foundation, revealing how it can assist you in cultivating subtle body awareness. Becoming aware of inner stillness is life-changing, as it opens the door to potentials, possibilities, and countless spiritual faculties, such as various psychic abilities and the expansion of one's consciousness to the greater reality of spirit. A powerful, high-vibrating experience, the awareness of inner stillness shifts you to a version of yourself where the chakras are free-flowing and energized, unlocking their tremendous potential to heal and restore you.

With greater discernment through stillness (awareness of inner silence) comes the ability to become aware of the subtle body on a deeper level. The ability to discern comes with the recognition of one's spiritual nature and the light body that emanates from it. In other words, acknowledging who you are spiritually shifts you inward as you reflect, allowing you to resonate, feel, and directly experience the soul and all that is within it. Coming from this new and clearer vantage point, you see yourself with clarity, understanding that you're not a physical body but have one, and that you're not the ego but have taken one on for the purpose of being human.

This expanded awareness is the superpower of all superpowers, as it brings you the remembrance of your oneness with Source and all of the clarity, wisdom, understanding, and discernment of a thousand lifetimes. It's the state of enlightenment—the return to the multidimensional Self.

Balance Begins Within

Your vital energy is your spiritual currency, in a sense. It needs to be spent wisely. When operating optimally, it gives you the right amount of current, or energy, and desire to spring forth out of bed in the morning and tackle the day with vigor, strength, and determination. Left to the control of outer forces, or at the mercy of reactivity or circumstances, our vital energy can become blocked, leaving us feeling not at our best. This is why inner balance is important, and it begins by paying attention to what the mind, body, and soul require.

The mind, for optimum health, requires balance between negativity and positivity, as well as direction to direct our energy toward something, whether it's work or accomplishing a goal. The soul sets the vision (its desires), but it also wants to be remembered, actualized, in fact, by you becoming aware of it. This is achieved through the mind's inner balance and calmness, which offers the clarity to recognize inner stillness. Working with these aspects of yourself harmoniously, the body can be given the right amount of appreciation and correct nutrition through greater self-awareness, filling it with energy and vitality. All three aspects, when being tended to and combined, create inner balance. And from the space of inner balance and stability, you can extend that mental sure-footedness toward your own life, in all its facets.

Finding balance in your outer world, in work and play, with regard to helping others and your relationships, is a conscious decision. We can't really be of help to anyone if we're running on fumes, drained, stressed, and constantly tired because we've forgotten to look after ourselves first. Creating healthy boundaries and priorities by being in touch with how we really feel and honoring that is how outer balance is achieved. In other words, be self-centered, not in an egotistical way where one takes and takes but rather in a conscious, balanced way by recognizing that one can only really give their best when they're centered, strong, calm, and wanting to give of themselves.

Many of us have become "people pleasers" out of the fear that if we say no, we'll be judged and looked at from a different light. But here's the thing, we're really not responsible for other people's happiness, and we can't control how someone else perceives us.

Learning to look after yourself first by having boundaries and knowing when to say yes or no begins the process of restoring your self-worth. You're valuable as you are and worthy enough to not spread yourself so thin that you're left feeling exhausted and resentful. Boundaries can be developed through many ways, starting with clear, honest, and effective communication. They can be cultivated by practicing becoming assertive, as well as by giving yourself permission to say no to the things that don't resonate with you. These approaches are based in mind-body awareness and self-responsibility (recognizing that no one else is responsible for maintaining your inner state of being but you).

Ten Tips for Setting Healthy Boundaries

Let's look at ten more ways to cultivate healthy boundaries. These tips will help protect your vital energy. These are simple insights and ways that will pay back in dividends in the form of inner peace, increased energy, and happiness.

- Make time for yourself. Set aside specific amounts of time, or an entire day, for yourself and your needs as you feel necessary.
- Cultivate the practice of letting go of guilt. It's okay to look after yourself first. More than okay, in fact.

- Become aware of energy vampires. These are people who mostly take. Some are unaware of how their neediness impacts others. Awareness is everything in this case. And it's up to you to decide what your limits are.

- Make a list of priorities and move from there. Realize what's most important and where your energy is most valued.

- You don't have to respond to everything immediately. Not every situation is a fire, requiring an instant response.

- Be prepared for reaction. Not everyone will be happy with your decision to have boundaries, and that's okay.

- You don't have to overexplain yourself. Nor do you have to over-apologize for practicing self-care.

- Continue to practice self-love and self-worth through positive affirmations.

- Have a healthy perspective on your boundaries. It's all about balance and following your intuition.

- You can be flexible in your boundaries. Exceptions can be made, as you see fit. Flexibility, like with anything, is key.

Chapter Three
Why We Experience Dis-ease

I have come to understand, through personal experience, reflection, and insights, that we, as souls, choose a variety of challenges and adversities before coming into this reality. We do this in order to fully immerse ourselves in the human experience. The main reason is for creating enough inner contraction of energy and emotions (suffering) to create the right atmosphere for personal growth and evolution of consciousness.

We don't go through personal problems because we're weak, lacking in something, or being punished. The challenges we experience are just a part of being human. We choose to forget our spiritual nature, take on a human persona, experience the range of emotions, and feel contrast in order to decide what it is that we prefer.

In the spiritual realm, suffering and limitations are nonexistent. The soul may have a concept of suffering, but without experience it's just an idea. Hence the decision to experience the world of seeming opposites and relativity—up, down, hot, cold, sickness, health, and so on.

To make sense of why people experience the health challenges they do, one has to come from a spiritual perspective, an elevated point of view. The soul knows who and what it is. It knows it is eternal, limitless, and can achieve and accomplish anything with desire and intention. It also knows that this experience we call life is temporary and temporal in nature.

There are times when a soul will choose what may seem to be a harder or more difficult health issue because that soul has a specific plan and purpose for itself. Understandably, when one is in the midst of a health crisis, it's hard to see the purpose or even the blessings that come with such a trial until one is on the other side of it.

Generally speaking, all adversity can offer some, if not all, of the following lessons, reminders, and gifts, such as:

- forgiveness
- the opportunity to love ourselves and others
- nonattachment
- the remembering of the present moment
- a path to become fearless
- the gift of personal growth

Serious or life-threatening illnesses remind us of the temporariness of this experience, how important it is not to sweat the small stuff, and the value in forgiving ourselves and others. They remind us of the preciousness of our lives and how important it is to extend love and kindness to ourselves and the people in our lives because people will remember not so much what you did but who you were as a person and what you embodied.

When someone is faced with their mortality and the fleetingness of life, they're being guided to remember the art of nonattachment. Nonattachment allows one to let go of the need to control, shifting the person into the flow (the forward current of life) rather than trying to swim against it. Nonattachment is not giving up but instead letting go of resistance and stepping into grace.

Present-moment awareness—and this ties into becoming fearless—gives us the relief of higher-vibrating energies based in spirit as opposed to the heavier energies tied to the past and the future. Realizing that the present moment is all there ever really is gives one the clarity to see the concepts of past, and specifically the future, as it relates to fear. Understanding that fear is based in the uncertainty found in the future, one can choose to anchor themselves into the safety and strength found in the now. As one begins to become aware of and cultivate these insights and spiritual gems, the result is personal development and growth through self-awareness and understanding.

I would also like to add that personal adversity is an opportunity to cultivate the powerful forces of faith and trust. When developed and remembered, these two words become reality and timeline-shifting allies, especially in times of need. I would also be remiss if I didn't mention that when refined, faith and trust allow you to let go of the how and when. In releasing expectation on a specific result, we untie the universe's hands, allowing for something even greater to be manifested in our experience.

Sickness as a Catalyst to Awaken

Illness, even a serious, life-threatening diagnosis, doesn't have to be a death sentence. Decision combined with the strength of one's desire and will to overcome can shift one positively and set the stage to transmute the suffering of dis-ease. This can become a catalyst for a shift in consciousness (an awakening) and the healing that comes from it on all levels—mind, body, and soul.

Like any other life challenge, sickness has the potential within it to become the fire that lights the fuse for transformation. The truth of the matter is that change never happens when one is comfortable. Our strength and determination are forged amid adversity, and a health challenge is most certainly that. When your back is pushed up against the wall, know that you're not at your weakest because if you're ready and open to universal assistance through desire, intention, and, ultimately, surrendering it all to Source, that's where you actually may find that you're at your strongest.

Dissolving the Fear of Sickness

The root of the fear of sickness is based in three things: not understanding what fear really is; being disconnected from the idea that mind, body, and soul are one; and the belief in the uncertainty that comes with the future.

When the thinking mind is left unattended, wherever or whatever one's attention is placed upon is usually what's repeated and amplified by the egoic mind. The ego—by its very nature—repeats, expands, and even darkens (to a certain degree) what it becomes aware of. In doing this, it creates limiting ideas, including fears, surrounding whatever it's focused on. Sometimes these fears are more in the background (subconscious), and others are more pronounced, seeping into the conscious mind and creating fear when we give the ego our belief and react to it.

Having shed light on how fear operates, let's further shed light on it—revealing what it really is relative to your spiritual reality and inner stillness. Fear is not real and is not a reality to those who understand who they are in stillness. It may still be experienced to one who is stillness (aware), but in knowing that fear is sponsored by the ego (the dreaming state), one sees fear-based thoughts for what they are: distortions relative to the truth of inner stillness. Understanding that fear is always sponsored by the false, or shadow self—and that it's illusory—alleviates some of the seriousness that fear projects, ushering in relief.

You don't have to fight or resist fear, but rather see it for what it is through the clarity that's offered by the present moment. Reaction is what perpetuates fear; observation and nonreaction starves it. As you practice the art of nonreaction, the ego will have no choice but to loosen its grip on your consciousness. It may, as you awaken more and more, throw the occasional tantrum and even seem louder at times, but that's because you're becoming more aware of it. Remain calm in the knowing that as it is losing its power over you, you are reclaiming yours.

The concept of mind, body, and soul being one is based in direct experience from my point of view. I was reminded by the subtle body that every cell is always listening, and I understand that self-responsibility is required to dissolve negative emotions such as anger and fear as they arise. This takes the practice of being present as you navigate your day, preferably moment by moment. This is accomplished by consciously reminding yourself of the present moment and to observe and then challenge negative thoughts as they present themselves. Be mindful that the practice of being awake and alert is a lot simpler and exponentially more empowering than the alternative of operating through ego, or third-dimensional consciousness. "Is this thought or emotion serving me?" is the question to ask, which by virtue will lead to your answer.

I also want you to be mindful that when fear attacks—whether it's your well-being, relationships, finances, or health—you have time to choose a different thought and a higher-vibrating feeling. Being in this space-time experience through the manifested world affords us the time to choose an alternative, more empowering and desirable thought and experience. Just because fear has popped into our heads, and even if one has temporarily reacted to it, doesn't mean it will come to pass. Yes, our thoughts and emotions are doorways to potential realities, but choosing consciously and differently in the moment shifts us into a higher and more aligned timeline, or positive future reality, through the now. When choosing a different conscious thought and higher timeline, the key is to do so not out of fear but from the power of your will to choose that which you desire.

The belief in the mind construct that is the future automatically comes with the feeling of uncertainty. Leaving our destiny in the hands of the egoic mind's future projections, we're left often experiencing confusion, indecision, fear, and a lack of clarity. Bringing your awareness back to the safety and clarity of the present raises your awareness toward the fearlessness of the soul, allowing stillness and intuition to guide you.

The future, like the past, can only offer you what they are: lower-vibrating energies relative to the clear and high frequency experienced in the now. Understanding what the future really is can transform it from being a source of suffering and anxiety to a reminder to come back to the strength, ease, and peace of the only instant there ever is: the eternal moment of now.

Death Is Transformation and Letting Go

Having touched upon the idea of death, I found it important to offer a deeper spiritual point of view regarding this subject for one who is physical body identified. Death can be viewed as nonattachment (letting go), as to allow for renewal of mind and personal transformation. Death is nothing to be feared but rather understood, as it leads to personal freedom and mastery.

Relative to the eternal nature of life and of consciousness, death is a concept and, ultimately, an illusion. The physical body is not who you *are*, but what you *use*. Animated through the subtle body via the power of the soul, the body is simply matter brought to life. It's a space suit you take on, just as you take on an ego, to navigate the manifested world. It's a temporary disguise to hide our true selves from each other while playing the temporary game of separation. This is not to diminish the physical body or take away from the human experience in any way, but rather to offer insight into the reality of our eternal nature while revealing the temporary experience of being human.

Death can be viewed from an expanded awareness as the act of letting go. Whether it's letting go of an old, limiting belief or the physical body when the time comes, death in each circumstance is the taking away of your energy from something that is no longer serving you. In that process, it allows for coming into greater awareness and more into your true, spiritual self.

Death can be defined as the art of practicing nonattachment—the art of letting things die in an energetic sense. Mastery is knowing to let things go on a moment-by-moment basis. One operates consciously by letting negativity die as it arises through observation rather than reaction and letting moments die so that you can come into a new one. Use death to your advantage when manifesting is done by allowing the past to die and laying it to rest so that a more desirable and intentional present moment can be aligned with. Finally, allowing the ego to die, moment by moment as you let go of who you thought you were in thought and emotion, is how you renew your mind and resurrect the soul. As darkness is laid aside, the light within rises.

Looking at this concept clearly from a spiritual perspective, death is a process that leads to personal transformation, energetically speaking. As a part of life, it leads to renewal and rebirth. At the moment of one's awakening, the third eye is activated and signals the soon-to-come experience of ego death. Having gone through that ego death, that experience of "dying before you die," I can assure you that the process had no sting whatsoever. It's that initial ego death that teaches and affords one the awareness to live masterfully—attached to nothing, while being able to enjoy everything. I would also add that one's third eye awakening and the ego death that follows is an act of grace that cannot be forced; it can, however, be welcomed through desire. Source Energy—that which is within all of us—knows the perfect timing. If and when one is ready to lay aside that which no longer serves them (the ego), they can step into the next grandest version of themselves.

Ego: Universal Energy Disruptor

Now that we've had a general overview of the spiritual purpose of dis-ease, we're going to look at it closer by focusing on the source of fear and dis-ease itself: the ego. The ego, as I've mentioned, is the shadow self and the contrast to our light because of its lower-vibrating energy. If we're really wanting to understand what perpetuates dis-ease, what has us continually experiencing not only health issues but also problems in other areas of our lives, then we have to become aware of the following: ego identification, which includes the belief in the reality of the mind constructs of past and future, is how this is allowed to happen. Because of its reactive, contractive, limiting, and repetitive nature, the ego cuts us off from universal energy and its flow, impacting us energetically through our chakras, when we unconsciously react to it rather than respond to it consciously.

Let's look at how universal energy is affected. The soul, with its high-vibrating field of energy, extends the same to your mind while ushering in expansion of consciousness, healing, and balance through the stillness found in the present moment. The ego's purpose is the exact opposite. The ego contracts your energy, making you feel small and separate, stifling your energy centers (chakras), and blocking healing by operating backward, or contrary, in its energy and thinking, relative to the forward flow of life. This is its nature because the ego, in and of itself, is a dream—a belief in separation from creation itself. It's this one sponsoring belief that one is separate from Source that gives birth to all the limiting, contracting, and energy-draining thoughts and emotions that follow. With this foundation of understanding why the ego operates the way it does, we can move forward with greater clarity as to how it achieves its goal of disrupting one's flow of universal energy.

The ego, in essence, is the past and the future disguised as thoughts, emotions, and even memories. Attempting to create a reality separate from Source, from life itself, the ego ignores the reality of the present moment because that's where universal energy abounds freely, always in a vertical, ascending manner, while the ego operates in a back-and-forth, linear fashion. It's this back-and-forth motion (the continuous living in the past and then having it repeated through projection into an illusory future) that keeps one stuck, or stifled, energetically speaking. When someone says "I feel stuck," they're expressing what they're literally experiencing internally—blocked energy wheels, or chakras, as negative energies are accumulated and repeated—all sponsored by the ego.

As a side note, this all made so much sense to me several years back when the subtle body revealed these insights surrounding the concept of feeling stuck. For years before my awakening, I often felt stuck, like I wasn't moving forward, never realizing or understanding that it was my chakras being affected by negative energy through reaction, based in strictly past/future awareness, and the negative energy accumulation that comes with operating that way. I would quite often say back then, "I just want to get unstuck!" We'll be discussing how to become unstuck in chapter 4, and I look forward to sharing those insights.

The ego is fear because of what it is and what it offers, or projects. Dark by nature, the ego can only give one what it is: unease, in essence; the anxieties that come in the form of attachments; and thoughts of anger, frustration, worry; the fear of lack, loss, the fear of sickness; and, yes, even the fear of death. To be clear, these thoughts, or nightmares, are not the problem in and of themselves but rather as the belief and identification with these thought forms, which become energized and brought to life in our minds, through reaction.

The ego creates a fear, plants it in one's mind, and, if one is unaware to what it's doing, will be watered with reaction, expanding that fear, making it look bigger than it really is. This is how the ego hijacks one's consciousness: fear is presented, the person reacts because the feeling is undesired, the fear balloons in the mind through reaction. While one is reacting, they're feeding the ego with their vital energy. This is also how it perpetuates itself in one's consciousness, and why so many people are often feeling drained and exhausted—their vital energy is not only being expended but is also being cut off due to ego identification—identifying with the thinking mind.

What I want to make clear, as I bring this discussion to a close, is that without your belief and reaction to what the egoic, thinking mind is offering you, it can actually do no harm to you. The ego needs your faith in fear—*in it*—to take its thought forms and possibly manifest them into a physicalized experience. The key is to starve the ego of your belief, take away your faith in fear, and see it for what it is: the dreaming state of thought. This is what shadow work is all about—looking at the darkness consciously and facing it, so that it can be transmuted and released to allow healing and the experience of wholeness to return.

The Purpose of Fear

We live in a world of relativity, one of contrast. In a world filled with opposites, everything seems to have its contrasting counterpart. In a sense, the ego, which is fear itself, is the contrast to our inner light of consciousness, of stillness. Fear is the absence of light; it's the darkness we experience as anxiety, worry, doubt, uncertainty, and, when allowed to run amuck, can evolve into dread.

A necessary part of the human experience, fear gives us the experience of contractive energy and a taste of what it feels like to endure suffering—all of which are necessary to make a shift in consciousness and awaken. Often misunderstood, fear is actually a messenger, telling us that we've come out of alignment, out of the present, as too much attention has been placed on the uncertainty that often comes with the idea that is the future.

From the subtle body's perspective, fear is illusory in nature from a spiritual point of view, but it is experienced as one's personal reality when belief is given to it, bringing it to life. Because fear is illusory, it cannot evolve—one cannot change its nature, you can only perceive it differently through greater awareness. Looking at fear and hoping it will change or that it will stop, will not disarm it. Fear requires your conscious awareness of it, the understanding that it's the dreaming state and ultimately not real, relative to the reality of inner stillness—which is your core beingness.

Of course, there are times when fear serves its purpose, and one should heed it. For example, fear would tell you not to jump into a river that is crocodile infested, for obvious reasons. But fear on a day-to-day basis—that is contracting, keeping you stuck, and preventing you from achieving your desires—is the fear that's being addressed here. It's the fear of lack, loss, and sickness that requires one's conscious awareness and needs to be tended to.

The ultimate purpose of fear is to serve as a catalyst for one's awakening. As it grows over time disguised as negative emotions such as anger, worry, or any other lower-vibrating emotion you can think of, fear, when left unattended, layers itself over one's consciousness. It's this buildup of negative energy that creates an emotional heaviness and the pain associated with it. This accumulation of negative energy is what causes one to contract, energetically. As it does this, it's also setting the stage for the possible moment where you decide you've had your fill of fear and its density. Like an elastic band, the further you go back in negative emotion, the further you will propel forward in consciousness when you finally let go.

The instant you bring your awareness fully to the dreaming state of fear is the moment when you'll shift toward the possibility of a spontaneous awakening: third eye activation. The third eye is a spiritual force located in the forehead, and once activated, the third eye has the power to shut down and silence fear, leaving you with the clarity and peace of a silent mind.

Post-awakening, one will still be able to experience the contrasting energy of fear. However, with the clarity of the third eye, you'll no longer react to it, as fear has lost its teeth. Instead, you'll respond to it with the knowing that it's not real, now using it as a reminder to come back to the reality of the present moment.

When negative emotion, including fear, arises within your consciousness and keeps coming up, know that there's a message there. Anything that keeps resurfacing is asking to be looked at, forgiven, and released. Negative emotions are like energetic leeches in a sense; they'll keep coming back, draining you of your vital energy until they're faced and laid to rest. With an understanding of what fear is and what it's trying to convey, you can approach it consciously, in an empowered way that allows it to go from a source of one's suffering to a reminder to awaken and re-awaken as needed.

The inner balancing/neutralizing fear exercise I offered in chapter 1 is essentially one of the most powerful strategies I have to disarm fear through the clarity of awareness. I use the strategy to navigate daily life in a more confident, empowered way. With practice, it can empower you in the moment as you navigate your life.

⑥ Clarity and Discernment Exercise ⑨

I'm now going to offer you a simple yet effective awareness-building exercise that will have you cultivate greater clarity and discernment as it pertains to your thoughts. The goal is to become conscious when negativity or fear arises, so that you can approach it in a more mindful way. You're going to need a pad of paper and a pen or a pencil, or an electronic device.

Find a quiet space, free of distractions. Sit at a table or on a sofa, as long as you're comfortable. Have your note-taking supplies with you.

For the next five minutes, bring your awareness to the thinking mind, observing it without judgment. Just bring your attention to it. Write down what the egoic, thinking mind is offering you in terms of thoughts, and what it may even be trying to predict for you.

Once you've written down the thoughts, emotions, and possible predictions it's trying to make, look at each one for a few moments. Reflect on them, and then ask yourself the following questions:

- Is this empowering or disempowering?
- Is this positive or negative?
- Is this the past or the future being presented?
- Is this fear and anger, or does it feel lighter, like joy and happiness?
- Lastly, is this still serving me?

You can write down your answers or simply make a mental note. If you find that some of these thoughts, emotions, or predictions, are not in alignment with who you are, then approach them with the inner balancing/neutralizing fear exercise, where you observe and then challenge negative thinking, as you remember the present moment.

This is an awareness-building exercise, and I always say less is more when it comes to making positive, inner shifts. It only needs about ten minutes, and it can be done daily, or you can choose to begin with practicing it twice a week.

As you become more aware of your thought patterns and are able to discern when fear arises, disguised as the past or future, you'll be better equipped to deal with these energy-draining thoughts and emotions more effectively.

Chakra Attacks

I often say "awareness is everything" because it affords me the clarity to bring my attention to a particular facet of my life in the moment, whether it is regarding a relationship, a goal, or my health. Then, I can address the issue at an energetic level as it arises.

There was a time in my life when I was at the mercy of fear and the chakra attacks that were experienced as a result of energizing the attacks through a lack of awareness. Allow me to explain. When a negative thought is energized through reaction, it becomes an emotion and is projected outward. As the energy is externalized, it is immediately returned to its source, which is you, because we are, in fact, all one. In other words, you can't paint anything or anyone outside you in a certain way without instantly feeling and becoming what is being projected.

The emotion that is being projected determines which chakra will be impacted or blocked. All of this becomes more apparent the closer one shifts toward their inner being. Through inner stillness, one's core state of being is reflected as silence. It's unchanging, and any movement that takes place on the surface of one's mind is always transient, changing, and in motion, or e-motion (energy in motion relative to the unmovable nature of stillness).

Keep in mind that we're not being punished in any way when this happens, rather we're experiencing the mirroring effect of oneness—the inner and outer worlds are one. What we put out is what we get back. In identifying ourselves with the thinking mind and its emotions, we've entwined our vital energy with the ego, fueling and perpetuating it as it energetically impacts our subtle body and the energy centers, or chakras, within it through reaction.

When we project outwardly with negative emotion, such as anger, we only attack ourselves because on a spiritual level, you and that other person or thing are one. The feelings that are experienced during these moments are the density and darkness of the emotion with a counterclockwise or backward feeling of energy. This is what creates blocks in the chakras.

Understanding what's taking place on an energetic level when projection takes place gives us the awareness to choose to observe the inner/outer worlds, rather than reacting to them. All experience begins and ends in the mind. What we become, in any given moment, is what we experience.

The great thing about having this insight is that we can choose to no longer be at the mercy of projection, fear, or circumstances that appear beyond our control. You can choose not to react to the outer world, but instead bring awareness to the inner to tend to your own vibrational field of energy, thereby shifting from within, which will sooner or later be reflected without.

Common Projections

We're now going to look at some common projections/emotions and shed light on which particular one tends to be returned to which chakra(s) and impact it negatively. By bringing awareness to this, you become more conscious when it takes place and have greater understanding in order to alleviate any fear and confusion. This allows you to observe rather than create even more fear when it occurs. It's important to mention that there's nothing wrong with perception or being aware that someone else is experiencing it. In fact, it gives us the opportunity to extend compassion and understanding. What we're talking about here is the projection of negativity onto someone else and then continually repeating those thought patterns internally, allowing them to become beliefs. We're going to start at the root chakra and move up from there.

Root chakra: Projections/emotions of seeing someone else as unstable and seeing lack in someone else negatively impacts this chakra, leaving one feeling off balance.

Sacral chakra: Projections/emotions that include focusing on another's self-esteem issues, painting someone else as unattractive or ugly, or taking life too seriously will have an effect on this chakra, making one feel unattractive/undeserving.

Solar plexus chakra: Projections/emotions of anger, seeing others as victims of their circumstances, seeing weakness in others, and focusing on a hopeless world close off this chakra, separating the person from their personal power.

Heart chakra: Projections/emotions of anger, hatred toward someone else, and a lack of empathy; seeing others as being unforgivable; and refusing to forgive contract the energy of this chakra, closing one off from unconditional love.

Throat chakra: Projections/emotions of seeing others as fearful and recognizing a lack of confidence in another are energies that negatively influence this chakra. This unconscious action in turn impacts one's ability to effectively communicate openly and honestly in the context of relationships through projected fear.

Third eye chakra: Projections/emotions include overall negative thinking, seeing others as limited in some way, and focusing on the worst traits of others, which closes one off from the clarity of this chakra.

Crown chakra: Projections/emotions include believing that everyone and everything is separate in the outer world and feeling that you have to compete with everyone, which overshadows this chakra and the person from their spirituality.

As you reflect on these projections/emotions, you will find that, more often than not, these feelings are based in the past and are perpetuated by identifying and believing in the mind construct that is the future. Left unchecked, these negative emotions and projections start to dictate our behavior, leading us to make more consistent and unwise choices in the form of bad habits, such as poor food choices, as one seeks comfort. Projection can negatively impact the way we navigate our relationships—with people and even money—as one seeks external fulfillment in some other form, rather than finding it within.

For true healing to take place on any level, we need to first bring awareness (light to the darkness) so it can be looked at clearly through present-moment awareness, allowing it to be seen for what it is, so it can be let go as we realize these emotions are no longer serving us and are keeping us stuck. The goal is to be able to *observe the inner world of thought*. By doing that, we raise our inner awareness, seeing ourselves and others through clarity, through the silent witness, rather than the ego and its judgment.

We can start the process of neutralizing a self-attack and unblocking ourselves by choosing to see others through the present moment *as they are*—by realizing what they're experiencing emotionally is not who they are—replacing labels and projection with understanding and compassion. In the next chapter, we'll look at how to further become unstuck energetically and use the power of the conscious mind to direct energy and focus so that these emotional burdens can be released, allowing you to once again get back into the flow of things.

Identity with Past and Future

The fact that we experience the lower energies and densities of the past and the future are not the cause for dis-ease or uneasiness but rather identifying with these mind constructs. As one identifies and accepts the past and the future as reality, *as who they are*, they unconsciously bring to life the emotions, as well as the fears attached to those projections.

Left unchecked, these negative thoughts and emotions continue to hijack one's consciousness, rewriting the physical body's innate inner balance program. Being contrary to the infinite intelligence of the subtle body, because of its density and negativity, this negative program causes disruption within the mind in the form of resistance, which is then reflected in the body's cells and eventually can manifest as illness. Keep in mind that the past and the future don't have to be continuous sources of suffering or uneasiness, but instead, through inner awareness, can become reminders to awaken.

Becoming mindful of the reality of the present moment, the now, reveals the illusory nature of the past and the future. If the past and the future are mind constructs, then the thoughts and the emotions that represent them must be illusory, too. This is something that each person has to come to terms with and understand on a personal level.

Personal transformation and healing are an inside job, one that has to be directly experienced through inner revelation and insight. As we continue together in this journey, take what resonates and leave aside what doesn't. As awareness builds within, concepts that were once discounted can be reevaluated and then accepted, as one is ready to receive and resonate with it.

Negative Self-Talk

Coming from the expanded awareness that the physical body is a reflection of the mind, the realization is that every cell is not only

made up of consciousness itself but is also listening to you, await-
ing your commands—positive or negative. Our free will is found in
the fact that we can choose how to live our lives; that we have the
freedom to make of consciousness as we see fit. And consciousness, or Source Energy, being creative by nature, never says no. As
one thinks and speaks, one creates and becomes; calling forth reality through the infinite possible timelines that are available in the
unified field or unseen spiritual realm.

There are some less-empowering words or phrases that are used
unconsciously, through reaction, that impact the physical body initially on an energetic level. Allowed to be replayed in our minds and
restated through the spoken word, year after year, these limiting
and anti-health phrases can eventually become expressions of illness
that began as dis-eased thoughts.

The following six negative phrases need to be looked at more
carefully and consciously for the sole reason of their level of intensity, and where the energy is being directed. I'll also offer some
softer, gentler phrases that can replace these. As you look at these
six lower-vibrating phrases, compare their intensity to the alter-
natives being offered. Then from your own space of awareness,
decide what resonates with you as choices you would make.

Alternatives to Commonly Used Lower-Vibrating Language

- "I really hate…" alternative is "I dislike…"
- "Can't stand the sight of…" alternative is "I choose not to acquaint with…"
- "…makes my blood boil" alternative is "…doesn't resonate with me"

- "…makes me sick" alternative is "I am repelled by so-and-so's energy"
- "…disgusts me" alternative is "…isn't a vibrational match to me"
- "…is an idiot" alternative is "…is not as aware as…"

We are creative on every level, and we become energetically what we think, say, and do through action. Becoming mindful of our inner dialogue and the language we use raises our vibrational frequency as awareness is cultivated. Feel free to come up with your own gentler words and phrases to replace any conditioned language that you find negative and lower vibrating.

How to Digest and Process Anger

Apart from food and drink, human beings also ingest emotions, and often negative ones at that. Many of us are walking around needlessly carrying the burdens of anger, and it's only because we've forgotten who we are spiritually. In that forgetfulness, we have forgotten the destructive nature of anger—mentally, energetically, and physical speaking. Thankfully, there are ways to properly work through it, thereby digesting it, processing it, and releasing it to free ourselves and lighten our burdens.

We recognize the word *digestion* as the breaking down of food so it can be used by the body. In this case, there's an energetic spin being applied to the word, in that we can take anger and see it as an opportunity to evolve and grow, thereby changing it by processing it through inner action—from being a source of suffering to a catalyst for healing and expansion of consciousness. These two chakras are where anger and the attaching emotion of hate are often attached to: the solar plexus and heart chakras.

When we react out of anger, it's often because we're feeling helpless in the moment because of someone else's actions and because we can't control their behavior. Through that reaction, we become angry, allowing the anger to not only hijack our consciousness in that moment but also settle in either the solar plexus chakra or the heart chakra if left unresolved. The solar plexus chakra is responsible for our sense of personal power and the heart chakra is the center for love, compassion, and forgiveness.

Unhealed anger can set the stage for emotional issues—an imbalance of negativity—which impacts our mental state and our sense of well-being. This can spill onto our relationships and even our health, eventually. It can leave us in a defensive mode, or feeling on edge, ready to react.

The situation that gives rise to the anger dictates which chakra is primarily affected. A stranger cutting you off in traffic or saying something negative to you online will often trigger the anger that impacts the solar plexus chakra, as there's really no emotional or intimate connection between you and the other person. The ego and its pride have been insulted, and these energies are connected to self-identity and personality emanating from the third chakra. Anger that is sponsored from conflict from a more personal connection, such as a friend, a family member, a partner, or a spouse, tend to primarily affect the heart chakra, as one's feelings toward the other changes after the trespass. This shift in energy, and how you perceive the person who angered you, closes the heart chakra off to them in terms of love and forgiveness.

The way to approach anger, really in both circumstances, is to remember some key spiritual concepts and then apply them through awareness, forgiveness, and the practice of nonattachment, or letting go, to properly digest (break down the anger), process (work through it), and release yourself of this negative emotion.

Five Spiritual Insights for Understanding and Dealing with Anger

Here are five key spiritual concepts/insights to remember, which can then be applied to the simple exercise that follows in order to look at and heal anger, consciously.

- It's never really personal. When others trespass against us, it's not so much always about us, but instead about their own internal pain and anger that is being projected outwardly. When someone is projecting anger onto you, remember that they're really only attacking themselves, energetically, as they've forgotten that we're all one.

- Anger can be an opportunity to ask for clarity. When someone expresses their anger toward us, it's an opportunity to inquire and even self-reflect if there's something we did to invoke anger in the other. Anger can be seen as a messenger, not who the other person is. It could be highlighting something within ourselves that needs to be brought to the surface so it can be resolved. Remember that anger is often a passing emotion, and to continually see another person as always angry will paint them as such, even when they've moved on from the past skirmish.

- Being angry, and holding on to it, is punishment enough. You don't have to seek revenge when a stranger trespasses against you—they're already in the process of manifesting their own wake-up calls, which for them can become opportunities to shift beyond that emotion. In understanding this, you can choose to forgive and let go, understanding that the other person is suffering and is most likely boiling over, projecting the emotion outwardly.

- In a sense, anger is a possessive entity that hijacks one's consciousness, like any other negative emotion. No one really thinks clearly when they're angry—they can even seem unreasonable. Know and understand that the human being experiencing the anger, or negative emotion, doesn't fully realize what they're doing, as they've forgotten who they are beyond the thinking mind. Hence, we can come from a space of awareness not to take things personally.

- Lastly, holding on to anger is detrimental. First, energetically it can manifest in other parts of our lives, including our health. Understanding this, we can realize the value in forgiveness, letting go, and moving on from the vibrational frequency of anger.

⑥ Transmuting Anger Exercise ⑥

This exercise should only take eight to ten minutes. Find a quiet space, sitting or lying down is fine. Take a few moments, then close your eyes, drop your shoulders, and take a few deep breaths. Become present as you do so.

Once relaxed, bring your awareness to the emotion of anger within you. Look at the thoughts that have been sponsoring this emotion for a minute or two. Don't react if you can, but rather just observe them.

Then take two to three minutes to scan through your body and feel where this emotion is being stored. Is there a heaviness or a contractive feeling of energy in your heart or abdominal area? Is there any anger felt in the lower back?

Once you've identified the thought, the past experience, or the person that is sponsoring the anger, make a decision. Decide if it's worth keeping this thought and subsequent anger alive or if it is worth facing it and releasing it.

If you decide it's time to heal and release the thought and emotion, do the following:

As you focus on the thought/anger, declare the following: "I am no longer going to feed this thought with my vital energy. I will no longer react to it or identify with it. I am letting this go. This is the past trying to replay in my mind, and it's no longer serving me. I forgive (the person/event), and I release this energy and myself. I am letting it all go now."

Bring your awareness to the chakra that's been impacted by the anger. If it's the solar plexus, imagine the following for two minutes: See the word *anger* exiting from your solar plexus/abdominal area and dissolving as you release it. If it's been the heart chakra that's been impacted, see the word *anger* and *hate* if present, exiting from your heart/center of your chest, and dissolving as you release it.

Then for a minute or two, follow the next step for the correct chakra. For the solar plexus chakra, imagine it clear of anger, being yellow in color, happy and joyful, spinning clockwise at the perfect pace. For the heart chakra, imagine it clear of anger or any hate, being green in color, happy and joyful, spinning clockwise at the perfect pace.

The exercise is now completed. Take a few deep breaths, open your eyes, and come back to your surroundings. Give thanks for release and renewal. Use this exercise as needed to face, digest, process, and transmute anger, being mindful that what you imagine is taking place energetically now—in the moment—including healing.

How to Approach Dis-ease

If you're currently facing a health challenge, then this section was made for you. Having gone through my own health crisis, the one thing I intuitively knew as I was going through it was that I should not feed the dis-ease with my vital energy.

Keep in mind that it's our perception of things—how dark or light our outlook is through our thoughts, words, emotions, and reactions—that amplifies whatever is being focused upon in the moment. Nothing is so powerful or so insurmountable, unless we believe it so. Every part of you is creative, and you're always in the process of manifesting your reality. There are a few things to be mindful of, if one has the desire to heal and move past their condition, or a vibrational state (as I prefer to refer it), is being experienced.

Mindset is everything, and the decision that you will heal—coming from an awareness that you're already healed—is what makes all the difference, I have found. What I've also realized to be incredibly empowering is the cultivation of these four forces: desire, one's will, determination, and perseverance. As I gave life to these forward-moving spiritual faculties, I came from a space of non-expectation, as to how or when some type of healing was going to occur, but what I did have was the overwhelming will to live.

Desire (my initial spark) set the stage for me to invoke my will to overcome cancer. Desire is not a bad thing whatsoever; without desire, the manifested universe would not be. Desire is the spark of creation—the beginning of experiencing something different, a new reality. It's only our attachment to outcomes and expectations that snare us into suffering, so the key is to cultivate desire, become one with it, see it as a reality now, and know it's done but not be in any way attached to it.

With regard to one's will, it is vital to understand what I'm about to share. We've forgotten how powerful and reality-shifting our will is. Because the truth of the matter is that we share our will with Source. What you decide for your life is what Source decides for you as well.

I can tell you this, but really, you have to come to this conclusion on your own. If and when you do, you will have realized and activated a powerful spiritual force: the joining of wills, one that is in essence, unstoppable. Making the decision that you will triumph, that you will overcome, is what carves out and makes a way, I have found. The key to uniting your will with Source is to lay all the fear, doubt, and uncertainty aside. This, I have found, is what unties the hands of the universe, making all things possible, including spontaneous healing.

Being resolute that a way will be made and consistently operating from that space of awareness is what cultivates determination. Choosing that energy and the feeling that success is now can also strengthen you in your healing journey. The key is to not entertain a victim mentality—that will only sponsor and attract more of the same, such as fear and uncertainty. Rather, you have to embody the person who is already healed and whole—come from that space— think, feel, and speak from that vibrational frequency.

I want to briefly share a story of a man named Stamatis Moraitis, who was Greek but lived in the United States. I read about his story many years ago and have shared his story with many people as a source of inspiration. In 1976, while in his sixties, Stamatis was diagnosed with lung cancer by several doctors, and he had been told he had only nine months to live. Refusing conventional treatment, and due to the high cost of funerals in the United States, he decided to move back home to the island of Ikaria, Greece. Initially, his wife and mother tended to him. But soon, he reconnected with his faith, began spending time with old friends, tended to his garden, and made wine. Six months went by, and not only did he not die but he felt his strength returning. He watched his health improve as the years went by. Stamatis went on to live almost another forty years, passing away in 2013, not from cancer, and apparently outliving the doctors who diagnosed him.

What I gather from this story is that Stamatis, in making a decision, created a purpose for his life through sheer will and determination. Shifting internally was reflected in his outer world. He began living, and by choosing life, returning to his roots, and reconnecting with faith and community, he experienced something different and new. I can't help but feel inspired by his story and his life.

Understandably, being given a life-threating diagnosis can create a lot of fear, worry, uncertainty, and anxiety. But one doesn't have to remain in that vibrational frequency. Creating the desire to heal and live, carving a path with your will, being determined to see it through with nonattachment, and persevering when things look dark can shift reality and change things.

Perseverance is the spirit of choosing to move ahead, despite circumstances, despite what you've been diagnosed with. Spiritual awareness, knowing there's a higher power dwelling within you—that is capable of anything—is what takes a circumstance and converts it to an opportunity to transcend, overcome, and heal—returning one to wholeness.

Chapter Four
Healing Is Now

We're always operating with and from universal energy. However, the amount that we experience in the form of energy levels, vitality, and strength depends on one's level of awareness. Present moment awareness, the practice of nonresistance, and knowing the importance of letting negativity go are how we connect more fully with the endless supply of universal energy that is always flowing to us and through us. The subtle body, or light body, is what takes this energy and converts it through its chakras. We experience it as chi, or life force energy.

The flow of universal energy toward and through each and everyone of us never stops. It's always being offered, unconditionally, without exception. Consistent reactions based in having forgotten who we are, relative to Source, bottlenecks this flow.

When one is heavily ego-identified and operating primarily through the past and the future, the present moment—the doorway to unrestricted Source Energy—is all but forgotten. Getting caught up in linear time contracts one's energy field through thoughts and emotions. To be clear, as powerful and unlimited as Source is, it will not override what we're choosing. We're all powerful enough to cut off our own supply of universal energy by identifying as something other than who we are spiritually.

When nonresistance (choosing to be at peace regardless of what's presented before you) is practiced, you restore your vital energy as you starve the ego. That's how that works. Reaction is the thief that draws on your life force. As it does this, it energizes and perpetuates the ego. Thankfully, through inner work, one can get to a place where the ego has been so starved of your reaction that it can be diminished to the point where it can no longer hijack your consciousness with negative emotion. Instead, it becomes a whisper, reminding you to come back to the present.

One must decide whether to continue to fuel fear or cut it off from its supply through observation and nonreaction. Remember, the stillness within you is more than capable of dissolving negative emotion, regardless of its intensity. We're not talking about suppression whatsoever, but rather the power of unconditional love to dissolve anything unlike it.

What has just been discussed is but a glimpse of the transformative potential and power found within stillness. As fear is put in its rightful place, stillness is allowed to unfold and with it comes a greater flow of universal energy. With regard to letting negativity go, that ties in with the practice of being mindful—being aware when a negative emotion that no longer serves you arises so it can be looked at, consciously, and released through the understanding that if you were to identify with it, you would become it, allowing it to draw on your energy. Awareness truly is everything.

Knowing that universal energy is always flowing to us and through us means we only have to tend to our inner world and make the choice to allow ourselves to feel and experience the fullness of our inner being, and the overflowing energy it's constantly offering. Not only is awareness everything but so is alignment. What one identifies and aligns with is what one becomes, energetically.

Become Unstuck

At one time or another, many of us have said or heard someone say, "I just feel stuck." We are energetic beings, and when we've allowed negative emotion to accumulate, our chakras become impeded, even blocked, by the effects of replaying the past and then projecting a negative experience or emotion into the future, which is always done in the now moment. When we feel like we're not moving forward, it is experienced within us first, energetically, then projected by focusing on our circumstances. In other words, when someone is feeling stuck, they're literally stuck on an energetic level (at the chakra level).

When you approach a negative thought or emotion with awareness, with the presence of your inner being, and observe rather than react to it, you are in fact diffusing whatever emotion is being presented in that moment. As you consciously face particular negative emotions and fears, you are not only in the process of healing that particular energetic roadblock right then and there but you are also simultaneously beginning the process of clearing whatever chakra block has been in place from the past. By letting go of the dis-eased/ uneasy thought, by choosing not to charge it with one's vital energy, we let in healing and rebalancing energy.

Next to observing and challenging negative thinking, taking positive, forward-moving action alleviates the overall feeling of being stuck. Confused and uncertain feelings are messengers speaking to us to find inner clarity. If you've felt unsure of what direction you should be heading toward, or what your calling is, look no further than what your passions are and what excites you. Following your passion and doing what you love puts you on track to align with the soul's desires—what you truly desire.

Once you're clear on what it is you love to do, take the steps you can take and get moving. If you love painting, then paint and share your gifts with others. If you're called to be a writer, then write and share your talents with your audience. So many have the misunderstanding that all you have to do is vibrate with your dreams and align with them, and they'll just fall on your lap. There is some truth to that, but in order to come into the full manifestation of the desire, you have to marry the dream (the fifth-dimensional idea) with the third-dimensional (3D) reality by taking action. In other words, you have to embody the desire—in mind, body, and soul— becoming the very thing you wish to experience.

⑥ Becoming Unstuck Exercise ⑨

I want to now offer a simple exercise that will invoke the power of your imagination to envision yourself not only unstuck but also moving forward.

Find a quiet space and get comfortable. Close your eyes, take a few deep breaths, and just come into the moment. This exercise should only take four to five minutes in total.

I want you to imagine yourself standing in a beautiful park. The sun seems incredibly close and is shining. The temperature is just perfect.

Take whatever feelings and energies you've been feeling about being stuck (take a minute or two to collect them). Then, see them in your mind as being released from you. They are headed up and away from you, toward the sun. If you want, you can take the phrase "stuck energy" and use that as something you focus on releasing. Take a few deep breaths as you see yourself letting this energy go.

Watch for a minute or two as the stuck energy is absorbed by the sun's power, consumed, and dissolved by it. Drop your shoulders as a sign of release, and surrender that energy that no longer serves you. Realize you've just let that energy go.

Take a few deep breaths, let the moment go, and open your eyes, coming back to your surroundings. Give thanks for release and for becoming unstuck.

This exercise needs only to be practiced a few times initially, to clear one's energy field of the feeling of being stuck, perhaps two or three times in the first week. Use it as needed from then on to help clear any energy that accumulates that has you feeling like you're not moving forward. Remember the power in taking action, to merge your dreams and desires to the manifested world, which will shift you forward within and without in a very powerful way.

The High-Vibrating Frequency of the Now

Being the doorway to your spiritual nature and the spiritual realm that surrounds us, the present moment is incredibly high vibrating. It is so high vibrating that to be anchored in it through awareness is to become one with it and its healing effects. The energies are so powerful and light-filled that they consume anything unlike them; present-moment awareness illuminates the mind, raising your vibrational frequency to that of spirit, dissolving and casting out fear. Going with the flow, living moment by moment, shifts you into the ascending and life-affirming frequency that is universal or cosmic consciousness—inner stillness.

Through our changing thoughts, feelings, emotions, and outlook, we shift through different parallel realities countless times a day. As one shifts from within, positively or negatively, the outer world reflects those changes, often going unnoticed because of how subtle these shifts are. Through insight, we can decide to make more consistent and mindful choices—such as choosing to live more presently—as one becomes aware of the power and healing frequency of stillness that is experienced in the now. Through the present moment, one aligns with and vibrates closer to the soul and the dimension of inner stillness, which is unmovable, clear, healing, and predictable because of its unchanging nature, which is unconditional love.

When we're deeply aware of and operating through the present moment, we experience its clarity, as it's a reflection of the mind of Source. Through the now, we also create space between the mind constructs of past/future—allow for greater pauses of inner silence—as we remember our spiritual nature. Tapping into this spiritual awareness lays confusion aside, allowing the light information of stillness to flow freely through every chakra and then into every cell, organ, and system, filling them with light. The information found in the light of consciousness is the infinite intelligence that knows how to heal and restore balance within you—we just have to get out of its way, in a sense, by letting go of fear and letting in what's already present: stillness, which starts with the realization of the reality of the now.

When one is consciously aligned with the present moment, they are, in fact, embodying their spiritual nature (the soul) and because of that are in alignment with the subtle body and its divine intelligence. Being present-moment based, you have the clarity to detect, feel, and become aware of the wisdom and guidance offered from the soul, through the subtle body, to your conscious awareness (mind). And because of that, you'll be able to navigate your life, including your challenges—health or otherwise—in a more empowered and confident way, knowing that guidance is always available; one just has to go within, listen, and pay attention.

Through my own healing journey and personal evolution, I have found that being present has been incredibly empowering, restorative, and healing. It's my present-moment awareness that has allowed miracles to take place in my life, including spontaneous healing—on all three levels of my being. The doorway to the spontaneity of the soul, the now, offers unimaginable potential in terms of clarity, insights, wisdom, and the healing that extends from wholeness, of being one in mind, body, and soul.

Inner Peace

When we are at peace with ourselves, others, and the world, we're able to face challenges with greater confidence and manage stress more efficiently. In fact, when you know and have a baseline understanding that your inner being is peace personified, you have an inner compass that can lead you back to center whenever you're thrown off-kilter due to abrupt life changes or adversities.

I also want to mention that it is possible to enter into such a deep state of inner peace that the things that once got you worked up and emotional are no longer able to move you internally because of the profound stability offered through the peace of stillness. Let's define inner peace, reveal how it can empower you, and offer you ways to cultivate it, so that you're better equipped to navigate life through self-awareness or awareness of your core state of being.

Inner peace is independent of the outer world, as it's a reflection of the soul, your inner being. Unmoved by fear, or even the outer world, the inner peace I'm describing is attached to nothing—it is unconditional by nature. Inner peace is the direct experience of inner stillness combined with the awareness that the present moment is all there ever is. Not only is it the absence of fear but it's also the awareness and ability to transmute fear as it arises.

A centered state of being, inner peace is the result of knowing who you are beyond the thinking mind and knowing that you and Source are one. Through this high-vibrational frequency, fear is dissolved as it arises—through observation rather than reaction. In other words, inner peace affords you the strength to experience anxiety, even suffering on the surface of your mind, but because you're so at one with your inner being, you're able to be unshaken by the ebb and flow of the thinking mind. When you're at peace, you're clearer, able to focus, and can make decisions from a more stable and centered state of mind—allowing solutions to problems to arrive sooner and with greater ease.

To cultivate inner peace and allow it to blossom fully, one has to develop their awareness of the now and become mindful of these fear-dismantling forces: faith, trust, and recognizing the power in surrender (in letting go). Through contemplation of these spiritual concepts and introspection, we open the door to experiencing these spiritual allies in a greater way, as awareness brings things to life. Even reflecting briefly on a prior difficult time in your life, where there didn't seem to be a way but a way was somehow made, can assist you in developing faith and trust—in Source and in life—rather than giving it away to fear, doubt, and uncertainty. In other words, we always have faith and trust in something—and it comes down to these choices: the light or the dark. Choosing to let go of fear and worry, deciding to surrender, releases you of inner conflict, allowing you to get more into the forward flow of life. Shifting into this non-attached state brings you into greater alignment with your inner being and the peace that emanates from it.

Ten Mindfulness Tips for Inner Peace

I'm going to now offer ten tips to assist in cultivating inner peace. These insights are aimed to simply point you inward, reminding you that inner peace is an inside job that pays in countless dividends as you work at it through the development of self-awareness. Following these tips, I will provide a simple, guided meditation on inner peace.

- Remember the present moment throughout the day. Putting little reminders on the fridge or on your desk at work can help you be mindful of the now.

- Take a few minutes a day to reconnect with your inner being through meditation or quiet self-reflection.

- Practice bringing awareness to the thinking mind, recognizing its pattern of past-future. This will cultivate further awareness and clarity in knowing who you are, relative to the thinking mind.

- Develop faith and trust by realizing that life and universal forces are actually for you, not against you. Be mindful of these two forces often, and choose to have faith and trust in yourself.

- Practice self-care, which includes healthy boundaries. In other words, know when to say yes and no.

- Cultivate peace within yourself through greater self-understanding; knowing what the ego is, relative to your inner being. One is fear and the other fearless; one thinks and the other is silent.

- Practice gratitude. Being grateful shifts you into higher-vibrational states, aligning you closer to your spiritual self.

- Understand others by understanding yourself. When you realize we've all experienced the conditioning and suffering that comes with the egoic mind, you can choose compassion over judgment.

- Understand the concept of oneness. That what we're being, and what feelings and emotions we're experiencing in the moment, is what is mirrored in the outer world. Inner peace sees peace. Oneness sees oneness. Separation sees a separated world. In other words, perception is everything.

- Remember to slow down and simplify. We make better decisions and connect with others on a deeper level, when we're more present and not so rushed.

⑥ Inner Peace Guided Chanting Meditation ⑥

This is a simple but transformative meditation with the aim to align you with the inner peace of your being. By using the power of the spoken word together with the potential of "I Am" through intention, you shift, becoming that which you're expressing, energetically speaking. This meditation needs only six to eight minutes of your time, and can be done daily or a few times a week, at the start of your day or at night before bed.

Choose a quiet space and get in a comfortable position, sitting or lying down. Close your eyes, and take four or five slow, deep breaths as you relax and come into the moment. Drop your shoulders as you start with your first deep breath.

Follow your breaths for a few more moments, as you relax further.

As you come into relaxation, repeat the following chant three times, slowly and with feeling: "I am inner peace. I am peace. I am one with the now."

Once you're done chanting, take another three to four minutes just being and soaking in the energies of the present moment. Feel the aliveness of your inner being. Become aware of and feel the calmness and peace that is found in the now. Remember gratitude as you do this.

Then take a few deep breaths, open your eyes, and bring your awareness back to the here and now, and your surroundings. If you feel inspired, give thanks for the experience.

Heal Your Relationship with Circumstances

The way in which we understand and relate to circumstances is what positively or negatively impacts our well-being. Depending on one's level of awareness, circumstances are a source of stress or an opportunity to choose differently through contrast. I'm bringing this topic to light because so many of us often get caught up and stuck energetically because of circumstances. Having a negative outlook not only perpetuates the cycle of suffering but also lowers our vibrational frequency, which is felt in the body as sadness, helplessness, frustration, and even anger. To change the way we see circumstances, we need to look at them from a spiritual point of view, through clarity and understanding.

Because of our human conditioning, we've learned to focus on the outer world and on the physical and to see them as concrete and very matter-of-fact. Automatically believing what the ego projects, we make real the emotions we feel regarding a situation, or circumstance, which in turn paints what we're seeing a certain way. There's nothing wrong with this because in order to have preferences and choose differently, we have to experience the apparent "opposite" in a sense. In other words, if you're experiencing a circumstance that doesn't resonate with who you've become, you can decide to observe it rather than perpetuating it with your attention and vital energy. This doesn't mean you ignore or bypass. It means that you can decide to see the circumstance differently, as being neutral. A circumstance, or anything in life, in fact, has no meaning, save the meaning we give it. Going one step further, circumstances do not matter—what really matters is your vibrational frequency, your inner state of being, because it's your inner world that reflects the outer.

Choosing to see a circumstance as neutral is how you empower yourself to shift beyond it, starting from within, which will sooner or later cause a change without. Looking at circumstances through observation and awareness, or stillness, reminds you that the outer world is actually not so concrete, but malleable, based on your thoughts, emotions, beliefs, feelings, intentions, and outlook. I want to impress upon you that everything changes when you first change, or shift, from within because life is mirroring your state of mind—your state of being.

Making peace with a circumstance, whether it's regarding where you currently are in life, a relationship, or even a health issue, is what withdraws your power and vital energy from it, restoring yours. This is what it means to be centered; your awareness and attention is firmly planted in your beingness, as you choose to observe the outer world rather than react to it.

This inward shift is so empowering, on so many levels. First, it brings you greater calm and peace of mind in the knowing that you're no longer at the mercy of the outer world. You know you can change it and shape it as you shift and elevate yourself from within. Secondly, with that greater sense of well-being, you're able to relax and be more comfortable in your skin. You have the clarity to make decisions, not out of fear or worry, but through clear-mindedness and focus. And thirdly, in being at peace with what the present moment is currently offering, you vibrate more and more with your spiritual nature, embodying more of your spiritual, higher self.

If you find yourself experiencing an undesirable circumstance, remember the following: everything is temporary, and in fact, temporal (experienced within the mind). No storm lasts forever. Outer changes can take place as you make changes within, starting with a fresh outlook. Nothing has any meaning except the meaning you give it—everything is neutral, until it's painted a certain way. You can change your circumstances by first withdrawing your attention and focusing on them, and then deciding what you'd prefer to experience next, aligning with that, and then taking the action necessary to marry the idea/dream/5D reality to your 3D manifested world. As you take a different inner and outer approach to change a circumstance, be mindful to let go of how, when, and what the change will look like—this not only unties the universe's hands but also allows the process to unfold more smoothly, with fewer roadblocks, energetically speaking.

To take all of this a little further, it's not so much the circumstance being changed but how you perceive it. As you energetically cut the cord, or attachment in this case, you allow the potential for outer change to reflect your inner shift. A great start is a gratitude mindset, which shifts you internally, allowing you to recognize things that are already in your life to be grateful for and things to come. Lastly, as you imagine and have a vision of the desired change, come from a space of awareness that it's a reality now—you just have to become one with the desire, feel it as a current experience, as a fact, as you water it with gratitude.

Youthful Energy through the Present Moment

We are, and present to the outer world, the energy we are inside. Old thoughts, ideas, beliefs, and emotions are expressed in the way we feel, speak, look, and interact with the world. Identifying with the thinking mind and with linear time, one will identify with their age rather than the eternal youthfulness of the soul. Every cell, being one with the mind, reflects what one thinks about themselves. One can choose to make the shift into the timeless dimension, the eternal now, allowing greater quantities of light, life, and vitality into one's mind and physicality, changing the way one feels and looks.

The secret to looking and feeling younger (*the present moment*) is the doorway to spirit and the real you, who is teeming with and emanates light, love, compassion, beautiful thoughts, and attractive, essentially irresistible energy. Operating through soul-awareness raises your vibrational frequency, aligning your mind with that of Source's, which sponsors thoughts based in unconditional love and beauty. Transcendent of the lower energies of anger, fear, and jealousy, for example, being soul-aligned clears your field of these darker, and dare I say, uglier, old energies from one point of view.

Ten Timeless and Youthful Affirmations

The following list has ten affirmations, sponsored from the timeless moment of now, that will assist you in coming into vibrational alignment with timelessness and a more youthful state of mind. These affirmations can be said first thing in the morning or throughout the day. Being higher-vibrating thoughts, don't be surprised if you find other youthful, timeless thoughts come to your awareness, being sponsored from this younger frame of mind.

- I am not a number, but youthful energy.
- I am light, love, and vibrant.
- I am in alignment with the timelessness of the now.
- I am playful, joyful, and happy.
- I am renewed, moment by moment.
- I am spirit, and I am whole.
- I feel and look younger every day.
- I am attractive and magnetic.
- I am unconditional love, and I feel wonderful.
- I am clear in mind, body, and soul.

Chapter Five
Energy Medicine through Intention and Application

Energy medicine is a field of alternative treatments that use intention while working with the individual's consciousness and the body's life force to clear energy blockages and restore inner balance. This type of energy work can be used by the individual through various forms of meditation, practicing forgiveness, and chakra work. It can also be done by a practitioner to an individual in the form of acupuncture, distance healing (where energy is transferred to the recipient regardless of distance), and reiki, which uses hand movements with the intention to guide life force energy to promote relaxation and restore balance energetically. These are just some examples of energy healing. Through intention and conscious application, you can release old, stale, and life force–blocking energies to step into the next highest version of yourself, energetically in mind, body, and soul.

Energy medicine works by recognizing that first and foremost, one is mainly made up of energy and is working with energy always, either positive or negative, all of which are encompassed by universal energy. Awareness of one's subtle body and the energy wheels within it combined with the power of the mind through intention and the healing potential of the soul via the light-filled state of inner stillness creates the possibility for healing to take place. Awareness opens the door to experience. In other words, being open and receptive, or nonresistant, allows the flow of healing (universal energy) to re-energize and renew one on the levels of mind, body, and soul.

You have the greatest pharmacy within you: the brain. When directed through intention, imagination, and visualization and backed by faith and trust, the brain can produce amazing results and relief, naturally. Of course, there are those emergency situations and more dire moments when allopathic medicine is needed, but what I'm focusing on is the mental states of fear and anger that sponsor dis-eased thinking, which lead to expressions of illness, as there is no separation between mind and body.

The brain can be viewed as a translator of psychic information, taking positive or negative impressions and manifesting them as feel-good chemicals, such as dopamine and endorphins, or stress-producing chemicals, such as adrenaline and cortisol.

The subtle body is reminding me as I write this, that just because someone has forgotten something, doesn't mean they've lost it. Many of us may have forgotten our potential, innate power to heal due to our human conditioning, but it's not lost. It's built in; the intelligence is encoded in every cell, in every aspect of your being. You just have to remember—remember who and what you are relative to the Source. The key is to use the conscious mind and direct it with the intended desire to impress your will upon the fertile ground of inner stillness: your higher mind. It also entails the willingness to go within and listen to the inner guidance and healing messages that are always being offered, as they are heard more clearly through the present moment.

Healing is a process, and the more one awakens, the more one returns to wholeness and the self-empowerment experienced in that state of being. We are energetic, spiritual beings first, and remembering this fact, one can begin to apply spiritual soul-utions in the form of directed energy medicine, forgiveness, and meditations. It all begins with awareness and the desire to heal—mentally, spiritually, and physically—into the next grandest version of yourself.

⑥ Energy-Healing Guided Meditation ⑥

I feel inspired to offer an energy-healing meditation, one that soothes and relaxes as it combines awareness and intention, which are catalysts for changing one's inner energetic state. With this meditation, I want to show how simply and quickly you can raise your vibrational frequency, shifting inward toward the wholeness of the spiritual self. This meditation can be done once or twice weekly, and it should only take five to eight minutes. Be mindful that what you imagine and speak is done now, in the moment, energetically, as you let go of how and when it will be translated in the physical world.

This meditation can be done in or outdoors, the important thing is that it's a quiet area, free of distractions. Get comfortable, sitting up so your spine is straight and your head is erect, or lie down if you prefer.

Close your eyes and take a few deep breaths as you relax into the moment. Drop your shoulders and let go.

After four or five deep breaths, bring your awareness deeper toward the body. Call all your energy and awareness inward.

As you're centered, imagine yourself as a being of light—ethereal, virtually see-through, emanating golden light from every part of you. Breathe slowly, in and out, as you imagine yourself as this light-being for the next three to four minutes. Feel the energy flowing freely throughout you, without restriction, as you see yourself being pure light.

Next, softly affirm the following, with knowing as you continue to see yourself in this energetic state: "I am healed now. I am light and love. I am healing energy. I am free-flowing energy. I am peace and harmony, which is reflected in the physical." Repeat this affirmation three times.

Once you're done reciting the affirmations, take a few deep breaths, open your eyes, and come back to your surroundings. Give thanks for healing and wholeness. Then let the moment go.

Forgiveness, Self-Love, and Acceptance

The goal of energy healing is to restore balance and invite wholeness back to the individual's awareness. This is the conscious unification of mind, body, and soul to allow wholeness to be remembered, gradually or spontaneously. Wholeness is an awareness; it's a state of mind, a healthy mind. A centered state of being, where a negative thought is balanced by positive thought and where the present moment is central to one's awareness instead of the past and the future, allows one's vibrational frequency to continually expand and rise up the ascension ladder that is the now.

Now that we've looked at wholeness from this perspective, let's look at some ways to unify ourselves using intention, guided by the mind to shift closer toward the wholeness of the soul, creating potential and possibility for that wholeness to be reflected in the physical. There are a few things to be mindful of when discussing energy healing. Because we are talking about energy, the mind, and the soul, know that these ethereal elements are not limited by time and space. These aspects of you are quantum in nature. In fact, being extensions of Source Energy makes the healing of even the longest-held emotional block possible.

Another thing to mention is that your level of belief, awareness, and state of allowing, or non-resistance, is what makes a new experience or reality possible. Healing of any kind is really about self-responsibility.

I want to emphasize the following: Forgiveness is a powerful spiritual tool that has the potential to not only heal the past and release it but also the power to reverse it. Having the strength to forgive ourselves, as well as others, is based in the awareness of oneness. The potential in oneness is unlimited. As one forgives, letting go of past trespasses, they shift into another parallel, an expanded version of themselves that is different from the person who was once angry—thereby reversing that part of one's past.

As many of us are already aware of, holding on to anger, grudges, or resentments for weeks, months, or even years is vital-energy depleting. It's draining because it disrupts the natural flow of universal energy that flows to you and through you. Choosing to forgive consciously frees the mind of the past, as it also clears up one's energetic field. But wait, there's more; it accomplishes even more than that. By letting the past go, along with all past grievances, one comes into a space of peace. It's forgiveness combined with the act of letting go that has so much healing potential.

The action of forgiveness is an inside job. Finding a quiet space and getting comfortable prepares you for the process. Forgiving oneself is a matter of self-reflection and then thinking or saying, "I forgive myself. I release myself. I am letting the past go." Choosing to forgive another is a similar process; it's a brief reflection of the trespass and then by thinking or saying, "I forgive you; I release you, and I am letting you go."

Having the strength to look at the emotional anchors that drag us down, such as guilt or anger, and choosing to release them is an act of courage, as well as one of self-empowerment. It's taking ownership of oneself and of one's destiny with respect to their life moving forward. Forgiveness is a healing force that is all-encompassing in terms of its releasing power to heal guilt, anger, and even hate.

Self-love, not in the egoic sense but through unconditional love, is a natural progression that follows forgiveness. Releasing the past along with its dark shadows allows for clarity to unfold, as one sees themselves clearer through the present. The start of reconnecting with your inner being is looking inward, and it no longer becomes a worrisome thing. There is greater calm, greater peace, and the potential to recognize the Self through stillness.

Self-love is choosing to no longer judge oneself. And when self-love is cultivated, projection is replaced with extension (compassion toward others). Remember that one projects, or extends, depending on what space they're in; through egoic consciousness there is judgment that labels the outer world. And through expanded awareness, we extend more of our true selves, allowing love to flow outward in greater amounts, as kindness and understanding.

Moving through the energetic healing process of forgiveness and self-love brings one's awareness to acceptance; of oneself, of others, and potentially, all of life, including one's current circumstances. This is where even more profound change becomes a possibility. Self-acceptance has the potential to heal the way we relate with others. Being in the space of acceptance is the state of being in positive, appreciative, forward flow, energetically speaking. One is no longer resisting "what is" in the outer but is instead in harmony with it and working with it. That's not to say you can't take action to change your life or a circumstance that no longer resonates with you, but I am saying that you can do it consciously without energetic roadblocks that often keep one feeling stuck, making transitions or life changes easier.

These three spiritual forces are powerful in their potential to transform us energetically from within. They can assist in bringing back inner balance, as one shifts closer inward by peeling back layers of emotion and conditioning. Keep in mind that nothing has to be added to you in your healing journey, but rather you must release the negative thoughts, beliefs, and emotions that no longer serve you.

Health-Affirming Sponsoring Thoughts

We've looked at the quality of negative thoughts—the uneasy thoughts that come with ego and physical body identification—and how limiting and reducing they can be. And we've looked at some general, life-affirming phrases. It's time now to look at twenty-two thoughts/phrases that emanate from the soul and higher mind that are soothing, expansive, and health-inspiring, based out of wholeness, or oneness.

A sponsoring thought or phrase is an originating idea that gives rise to and inspires more thoughts of the same. As you resonate with some or all of these ideas, you may find that other high-vibrating, health-inspired thoughts follow, creating positive momentum. Be mindful that on an energetic level, these statements are healing, as they uplift, feel good, and raise one's vibrational frequency. You can begin thinking and speaking these health-based affirmations today, if you feel inspired to. Ideally, they should be thought/spoken daily, a few times a day, to remind you and direct the energies within you.

Health-Affirming Phrases

- I am strength and vitality.
- This body reflects calm.
- I am gentle with myself and others.
- I am healthier with each breath.
- I love and accept myself.
- I am one in mind, body, and soul.
- I give thanks for perfect health.
- I am filled with light and love.
- Healing on every level is possible, and it is happening now.
- I am deserving of great health.
- I am more than capable.
- I am flexible in mind and body.
- Every cell is operating optimally according to infinite intelligence.
- I am powerful.
- This body is full of energy.
- I am releasing what no longer serves me.
- I trust in the body's ability to heal and restore.

- I am able to tune in to and work with the body's intelligence.

- I am heeding my body's nutritional needs.

- I am grateful and appreciative for this body and what it can do.

- I am resonating with the present moment in mind, body, and soul.

- This immune system is stronger than ever and is operating optimally now.

Every Cell Is Listening to You

Life responds to us—based on our beliefs, thoughts, words, feelings, emotions, and outlook—reflecting that which we're being in the moment. This mirroring effect is based in the spiritual reality of oneness, and this reflective experience doesn't stop in the outer world but is also reproduced in our inner world, as mind, body, and soul are one. Everything is consciousness, at its core.

Within a particular form of consciousness is an encoded intelligence for the full, vibrant expression of that particular thing. A plant is encoded to look like, behave, and function as a plant. A tiger is encoded to look like, behave, and function as a tiger. And human beings are encoded to look like, behave, and function as humans. However, a long time ago, through a collective decision to experience separation from our spirituality, humans have come to forget that life and everything within it, right down to every cell, responds to us. We've forgotten that we are the cause in our lives, and the effects are our manifested experiences.

The concept of cause and effect, in a spiritual sense, is a person's thoughts, attitude, emotions/feelings, and outlook that call forth an effect, or resulted condition. Understanding this concept has the extraordinary potential to shift one from feeling they're a victim to their circumstances to being the creator of them. If that's the case, then through positive, life-affirming inner action, one can make different, reality-shifting decisions as they raise their vibrational frequency, changing their thoughts, feelings, and outlook in the process.

Consciousness is within every part of us, manifested or unmanifested. It's who we are beyond the thinking mind; it's pure, undifferentiated potential. And it expresses what it becomes, be it in our relationships, finances, career, and, yes, health. The particular expression is based on one's vibrational frequency and the actions one does or doesn't take, as every part of us is creative.

For example, if one were to enter into a new relationship having not learned the lessons of the past one, one is set to repeat the experience, because one is still operating through the vibrational frequency based in the past. The energy that we carry and from which we operate from is what we come to experience as effects. As one shifts internally, in a positive fashion, one can potentially call forth similar energies in a partner, allowing for more harmonious experiences in the context of the new relationship. In other words, life doesn't judge what we should or shouldn't have, it only reflects our inner state of being. Source Energy, in a sense, is the producer and you are the director of your life; sifting, choosing, deciding, and becoming that which you desire to experience.

Our cells are consciousness themselves and reflect our inner state of being, positive or negative. Already encoded with everything they need to function optimally, our cells and health are only negatively impacted when there's an imbalance of excess negativity or stress in our lives that has become unmanageable. Fear, worry, confusion, and anxiety disrupt the flow of communication between the innate intelligence of the subtle body and the receiving consciousness within our cells.

Let's be mindful that there's ultimately a soul purpose in all of this. Forgetting who and what one is, is part of the process, so there's never any blame being given, whatsoever. It is necessary to know and experience what happiness is, as well as its opposite, sadness. To experience light, the dark has to be brought in. And to know and experience extraordinary health—in mind, body, and soul—dis-ease has to be experienced through separation and the forgetfulness that comes with it.

One can make positive shifts from within—challenging negative thoughts, realizing the present moment, letting things go, activating forgiveness—all of which are designed to release that which you're not (the ego and its fears), so you can embody who you really are: a light-filled spiritual being. It's the belief in negative thoughts that sponsor the fears and worries and confusion that energetically "tear one apart," creating separation within one. Wholeness is the return to centeredness—the unification of mind, body, and soul so they can function as they were intended to—as one.

As explained by the subtle body, extraordinary health is not only possible; it's a fifth-dimensional (5D) reality, already existing within each and everyone of us. It's experienced within the dimension of inner stillness. In this state, the thinking mind is quieted, silenced in fact, allowing infinite intelligence to direct the cell's activities, restoring one back to balance and optimal health. Being void of fear or worry, the strength of consciousness and its healing frequency fill each cell, organ, and system with light—the spiritual coding responsible for optimal health, clarity, wisdom, understanding, and healing. Through stillness, the fear of the ego is cast out, leaving the higher mind to communicate to your body's cells instantly, through knowing, through its vibrational field. The higher mind doesn't need to think how to heal, or restore, because it is healing and restoration, in essence. It is all that and more. Wholeness is a return to this awareness, to the present-moment reality of the soul and higher mind. You don't have to earn this awareness; you have to realize it by deciding who and what you are.

⑥ Cellular-Healing Guided Meditation ⑥

I'm inspired to offer a meditation that is geared toward consciously communicating with your cells and directing your vital energy to them, as to re-energize them and invite more light to them and yourself in the process. This meditation is only eight to ten minutes in length, and can be practiced twice a week or daily, as desired.

You're going to need a quiet space and a comfortable chair or area to lie down. If you're sitting up, your spine is straight and your head is slightly tilted toward your body. If you're lying down, just get comfortable, remember to drop your shoulders as you begin. Close your eyes, and take four to five deep breaths as you become present in the moment.

First, acknowledge the consciousness within you, the intelligence within, by thinking or stating: "I am aware of your reality, and I am aware that the consciousness within me responds to my direction." Do this with a lightheartedness, as you're sending gratitude toward your physical body, cells, and the intelligence within.

Spend the next four to five minutes sending love, gratitude, and appreciation to every cell. You can think or state: "I am grateful for every cell, for the work they perform, and for the healing potential within them." Repeat this three times slowly and with feeling.

This step is optional. If there's an area that's been in pain or giving you discomfort, bring your awareness to the area and send it love and gratitude while thinking or stating three times: "I am sending you unconditional love, light, healing, and nonresistance. I do not resist this pain/discomfort, but I accept it, and allow it to be transmuted in the presence of love now."

For the next three to four minutes, slowly affirm through thought or by speaking: "Every cell is functioning optimally, now and always. Every cell is filled with the light and love of consciousness. I am renewed now in mind, body, and soul. I choose gentleness, peace, and harmony, and I reflect that. I am vibrating in alignment with my soul and my higher mind. I am healed."

Take a few deep breaths, open your eyes, and come back to your surroundings. Give thanks for healing and renewal.

Energy Balancing and Healing via the Chakras

When we're centered and in alignment with our spiritual self, the chakras are able to flow freely, without hindrance. We're filled with energy and vitality, and we experience great health. Conversely, when we're primarily operating from our ego, we experience emotional and energetic imbalances, usually caused by some form of fear, which can impact a particular chakra center. Working with the chakras, we can let go of energy blockages, allowing balance to be restored.

The Root Chakra

The root chakra, when balanced, makes us feel grounded and stable. When we're out of balance with this chakra, we feel unstable, moody, and insecure. This energetic imbalance can spill out onto our relationships, creating strains within them. Like with anything, awareness of a root chakra issue can help guide us to a solution.

Connecting the dots and recognizing a root chakra imbalance can allow one to apply an energetic and mindful solution. Addressing and facing the energetic block, or fear, is a great start. Usually, it is caused by an unresolved issue from the past or some worry that is future-based, and becoming aware of the fear brings it to light, transmuting it.

You can begin balancing the root chakra through positive affirmations, such as: "I am balanced and centered" or "I am stable and secure." Be mindful that these, or any life-affirming or healing affirmations, are not looking at or based in the past. Instead, they are the potential and spontaneity of the soul, of consciousness itself. You energetically become what you choose now. You can also spend twenty to thirty minutes barefoot in nature, reconnecting with Mother Earth. Spending time outdoors in nature has an incredible soothing and balancing effect on our energetic fields; raising our frequencies naturally.

The Sacral Chakra

The next chakra moving up is the sacral chakra. Located just below the navel, this energy wheel reflects our sexual energy and creativity. When blocked, we experience a lack of creativity, passion, and sensuality. Positive affirmations to help balance this chakra include, "I am love and passion" and "I am creative by nature." Self-acceptance and self-love are keys in balancing this energy wheel and then extending that love to others, unconditionally. Tapping into your creative side and expressing your passions activates and opens up this chakra.

The Solar Plexus Chakra

Located in the upper abdomen, the solar plexus chakra is representative of our own responsibility and personal power. When out of balance, we can feel powerless, which can be tied to low self-esteem. We can counter these feelings with the following: "I am worthy" and "I am powerful and more than enough." Taking positive action, such as goal setting and living from the inside-out, can further assist in balancing this chakra.

The Heart Chakra

The heart chakra represents who we are in essence (love), and it's located in the center of the chest. This chakra governs our relationships, and an imbalance can lead to self-loathing and difficulty in relationships. Self-forgiveness and self-love through these affirmations, "I love myself unconditionally" and "I forgive myself and release the past," can raise our frequencies. Cultivating kindness and compassion can further heal this chakra and bring about balance.

The Throat Chakra

Located in the neck, the throat chakra is the center for our ability to self-express. When out of balance, we can experience timidness and a lack of confidence. Thinking and affirming the following can help shift us toward balance: "I am confident and fearless" and "I express myself honestly." Trying something like public speaking can help develop one's confidence while allowing this energy wheel to express itself more freely. Expressing yourself through journaling can also help open this chakra.

The Third Eye Chakra

The third eye, or sixth chakra, is located between the eyebrows. It represents clarity and intuition, and when it is imbalanced, we feel like a ship without a sail, unguided and lacking clarity and direction. Affirming "I am clarity" or "I am one with divine intuition" can begin to balance the energy. Meditation on stillness is a powerful practice that reconnects us and activates this chakra. Challenging negative thinking aligns with this chakra, energizing it, as you reclaim your energy in this process.

The Crown Chakra

Located at the top of the head, the crown chakra connects us to higher levels of consciousness and Source Energy. When closed off energetically, we feel disconnected and smaller than we really are. Shifting focus to "I am one with spirit" or "I am one in mind, body, and soul" reminds us of our connection to Source. Quiet contemplation of one's spiritual nature brings our awareness back to Source Energy, shifting us energetically to a more expanded state of awareness, as does the practice of observing thought.

Having a basic understanding of the chakras, and their energetic reality can help us understand who we are and how we operate. Everything begins in the unseen. Being insightful to our energetic aspects can help heal us and restore balance from within, allowing for the full expression of who we really are.

⑥ Chakra-Healing Exercise ⑥

The following exercise is aimed at bringing greater awareness to the chakra system, which will bring them to life and energize them, allowing for greater flow of universal energy. This exercise should only take about fifteen minutes, and it can be practiced once a week.

Find a quiet area. Get comfortable and close your eyes. Take three to four deep breaths while you drop your shoulders. On the last deep breath, bring your attention inward, starting with the root chakra.

As you focus on the root chakra area, send it feelings of appreciation and support. As you're doing this, visualize a red circle of energy flowing clockwise, freely, at a perfect pace. Do this for two minutes, then let go, moving upward toward the sacral chakra.

As you focus on the sacral chakra area, send it feelings of playfulness and lightheartedness. As you're doing this, visualize an orange circle of energy flowing clockwise, freely, at a perfect pace. Do this for two minutes, then let go, and move upward toward the solar plexus chakra.

As you focus on the solar plexus chakra, send it feelings of strength and power. As you're doing this, visualize a yellow circle of energy flowing clockwise, freely, at a perfect pace. Do this for two minutes, then let go, and move upward toward the heart chakra.

As you focus on the heart chakra, send it feelings of gratitude and love. As you're doing this, visualize a green circle of energy flowing clockwise, freely, at a perfect pace. Do this for two minutes, then let go, and move upward toward the throat chakra.

As you focus on the throat chakra, send it feelings of confidence and praise. As you're doing this, visualize a blue circle of energy flowing clockwise, freely, at a perfect pace. Do this for two minutes, then let go, moving upward toward the third eye chakra.

As you focus on the third eye chakra, send it feelings of recognition and value. As you're doing this, visualize an indigo (blue / violet) circle of energy flowing clockwise, freely, at a perfect pace. Do this for two minutes, then let go, moving upward toward the crown chakra.

As you focus on the crown chakra, send it feelings of being one with it and thankful for it. As you're doing this, visualize a purple circle of energy flowing clockwise, freely, out of the top of your head, at the perfect pace. Do this for two minutes, then let go.

The exercise is now complete. Take a few deep breaths, open your eyes, and bring your awareness back to the moment. Give thanks for awareness and inner balance.

Activating Imagination

Healing on an energetic level includes several modalities. It encompasses several different forms of meditation, reiki, prayer and forgiveness, light, and sound, including invoking our intention through our imaginations. In essence, any technique that harnesses universal energy in a positive way is a form of energy healing with the goal of bringing about wholeness—the realization of it and its expression of healing. Energetic healing begins on a quantum level, at the level of thought and imagination. What is held as true and real in the mind, or our consciousness, has the potential to be realized in our reality. The healing and improvement I'm focusing upon in this section is not only health but also the wholeness of you as a person—the other facets of your life: your relationships, state of mind surrounding finances / abundance, and career.

Using your imagination is changing focus, or shifting frequency, similar to changing the channel on a television. Every potential reality, or experience, is already existing in the unified field, or unseen realm, and it's your awareness of it that begins the process of bringing it to life. In order to really use your imagination to its fullest, you have to have a deeper understanding of who you are, relative to manifested reality, and how imagination can shift you toward the realization of your desires.

Here's some clarity regarding these three topics: You are consciousness operating within a greater/larger consciousness that's appearing as the manifested world around you, appearing as real. But nothing "out there" is real, rather it is a dream relative to the unchanging reality of inner stillness—your inner being. The outer world is not concrete but a projection of your focus and attention. By using your imagination, you can impress upon the higher mind your preference. The key is to feel the reality of the desire now, as you let go of any resistance or resentment to your current reality or circumstances. For without the opposite, you wouldn't have the option, nor the desire, to choose differently.

The focus here will be on the conscious mind and the third eye chakra, which will be backed by the reality-shifting power of the other chakras. Whenever we place an image in our minds, we are engaging the conscious mind through the third eye. The third eye is the channel between this reality and the unified field; it unites them through the oneness frequency of inner stillness.

Some things to be mindful of when using imagination are:

- As you visualize and see healing taking place, or a particular outcome, come from a belief (or better yet a knowing) that it's happening now, in the present, in real time.

- Come from a space of gratitude with your imagining; it amplifies one's visualization.

- Approach imagination, or any other intention for that matter, through non-attachment; removing expectation on the how or when allows universal forces to work without any imposed roadblocks.

- When you imagine, you are turning the ignition key to conscious manifesting; it starts the universal engine that creates.

- Let faith and trust overshadow doubt and uncertainty.

⑥ Imagination Development Technique ⑥

Let's now look at an imagination technique that employs the third eye and the conscious mind, as well as activates the other chakras during the process. Imagination is a powerful tool, and when developed it can assist in moving toward a positive direction in our lives. We've been given imagination in order to explore, to be able to choose, and to hone in on that which we desire to experience.

You can invoke and activate the chakras while applying the following guidelines during the imagination process to amplify feeling: Ground yourself (root chakra) in the image you desire as you immerse yourself within it. Feel the ease (sacral chakra) of experiencing the reality as you experience it expressing in your mind.

Remember the power (solar plexus chakra) of your consciousness as you hone in on the desired reality. Feel the joy and resonance (heart chakra) for the desire as being already fulfilled. Speak thanks (throat chakra) as you imagine the reality being here, now.

Clarify the image (third eye chakra) and include details while letting go of any conditions of how / when it will appear. Feel being one with the desire (crown chakra), knowing that what you desire for yourself is what the highest self, Source, desires for you.

Incorporating these concepts during the imagination process will amplify the signal, the desire, as you feel it as being already done.

⑥ Imagination Development Exercise ②

To begin, get into a relaxed position, preferably in a quiet space where you will be able to visualize without distraction for ten to twenty minutes, depending on how comfortable you are with the process. Once you're comfortable, take a few deep breaths, close your eyes, and bring your attention, your awareness, inward.

Take the next three or four minutes looking at the various aspects of your life—your health, relationships, finances, and career—and see if there's an area you desire to see change.

Once you've narrowed down where you'd like to see change, spend the next four to five minutes focusing on that particular area of your life and what positive, desired change would look and feel like. Here are some examples:

For health: Imagine yourself being healthy, strong, and vibrant. Create the positive feelings associated with being in that state. Feel the level of gratitude, now, as you see yourself embodying extraordinary health. See that image in your mind as being your current reality—choose it now.

For relationships: Imagine having harmonious, happy, and fulfilling connections with others. Feel the joy and gratitude, now, in experiencing those relationships.

For finances: Imagine what financial freedom would look like. See yourself doing the things you'd love to do—is it traveling or driving that dream car? Feel what financial freedom would feel like—as an abundant state of mind, now.

For career: Imagine doing the very thing that you're passionate about. Create the feelings and excitement associated with having your dream career manifested.

Once you're done imagining and focusing on an area in your life, shift focus to another area, if you wish. Upon completion of your intention, take a few deep breaths, let go of the image, and open your eyes. Give thanks for inspiration and for the desire fulfilled, as you let go of how and when it manifests in your life.

Practicing the art of imagination is a powerful way to not only focus your energy and clarify what you desire to experience in life but also aligns you closer to the third eye and the higher realms. This technique is a great way to move you forward toward realizing your goals, as it will also call forth other energies to further inspire you to take action, to marry the dream with physical reality. Like attracts like, energetically speaking. This technique can be practiced once or twice weekly, as you feel comfortable performing it.

That which you desire already exists in the unseen. It's up to you to align with it vibrationally by letting go of the resistance and allowing it to come to fruition in divine timing.

Remembering How to Flow

Life is like a forward-moving current, always moving in one direction. We get caught up swimming against the current, expending our time and energy when we're too focused on looking to the past, rather than being present, right here and now. Going with the flow is, in other words, the art of non-resistance.

With self-awareness, we can move through life with less effort and shift through inner roadblocks faster by practicing present-moment awareness; seeing the futility in hanging on to negative emotions that are based in the past; and remembering how one's energy, positive or negative, affects matter—the way one feels mentally and physically. In other words, knowing that life reflects our inner world, we can choose to see things as they are, without judgment or based on past data.

Chapter Six

Spontaneous Healing through Surrender

Before we dive into the healing potential found in surrender, I want to lay a foundation of what surrender looks like and give you a clearer picture of what to align with and what to let go of moving forward. The end of inner conflict brings all your aspects (mind, body, and soul) closer together as you come into harmony. Surrender is a powerful state to embody, as it unties the universe's hands, allowing one to vibrate and become more in alignment with their desires.

Imagine the following scenario: you're headed into battle against a dark, evil army. You think you're headed into battle alone, so you're feeling angry, frustrated, doubtful of victory, and afraid. You look across the battlefield and thousands of dark forces are lined up against you. It appears you're outnumbered. You're feeling the stress of the situation and resistance within you as the army approaches, thinking you're going to have to fight them off single-handedly.

As the enemy soldiers are about to descend upon you, you have an epiphany. You realize that although it appears this attacking army is outside of you, it's actually in your mind. In an instant, you realize the inner and outer worlds are one. And in that moment, you directly experience oneness with the entire universe, manifested and unmanifested. You've awakened to an unimaginable power and force within you, and it's Source Energy.

With this profound realization, you drop your weapons, knowing that you need no defense. You remember that you are connected with the most powerful force in the universe—the universe—and you are instantly equipped spiritually with gifts such as clarity, wisdom, and profound discernment. In that moment, you let it all go; all the anger, the frustration, the doubts, and the fear. You surrender. And by that inner action, you unleash a spiritual force the likes of which the world has never seen: the All That Is.

Suddenly, a clarion call is heard and an army of angels appears behind you, on either side of you, and above you. Their light is so bright, you can barely look at them. Then, in a flash, the light emanating from these otherworldly beings grows exponentially, consuming the darkness before you—the evil army has been dissolved by the power of their light. The battle has been won, and the power of light and love has demonstrated its faithfulness and strength.

The purpose in sharing this story was to make you aware of the difference between thinking you have to face life and adversity alone, versus letting go, trusting, and surrendering to the highest self within—Source Energy—and allowing universal power and its forces to guide you, strengthen you, and renew you in mind, body, and soul. We don't have to face our challenges alone; we have access to wisdom, clarity, and understanding. Life doesn't always have to be a struggle. Through spiritual awareness (our connectedness with Source) and surrender, we can lay aside our egos, the little self, and open the door to guidance and the highest self.

Surrender is letting go of the need to try to control the outer world, including outcomes, and trusting the built-in process that is designed for your life. It's the inner action of letting any inner resistance go so you can allow in that which you desire. As one surrenders, they begin to relax, a state that many of us are not used to. But it's that relaxed state, that nonresistant state, that allows you to vibrate at your natural vibrational frequency, putting you in alignment with your spiritual self. There's actually great strength and power in the surrendered state because you're not worrying if something will come to pass or not, you're not fixated on doubt and "what if it doesn't happen," which is based on an uncertain future. Instead, you're one with the present moment, knowing that your future is being called forth in the here and now.

Life is a process, an unfolding one. The most empowering approach to life is going with the flow—letting go of resistance through faith and trust. Pushing against life, resisting what is, complaining about how unfair life is, is how one remains stuck. There is a purpose in everything, even difficulty and adversity. In an infinitely intelligent universe, know that nothing is wasted—there are gifts and insights to be remembered through our difficult times, and nothing is in fact random, or happens by accident.

This is what surrender looks like: it's energetic alignment with Source Energy, as resistance and inner conflict has been laid aside. It's letting go of one's limits—the negative emotions that tie us to the past and try to limit and predict our future. It's giving every aspect of our affairs to the highest self—in a sense abandoning ourselves to universal forces through the realization that all of Source is for us. It's a process of emptying ourselves of negativity, moment by moment, so that we give the universe an opportunity to show us what's possible.

To clarify, surrender is trust that's been activated, as worry has been recognized futile because of its soul-crushing energy. It's an inner knowing that all is well—despite circumstances—and that everything always works out. It's a state of mind that doesn't have to strain in trying to figure out every step right now, but instead trusts the process, knowing that the highest self will reveal what steps to take as you take the first step forward. A merging of the local, and higher mind, surrender is the moment we lay aside our fears, as we decide to listen to divine guidance from within.

Inner Stillness Is the Unified Field

When it comes to healing, true healing, it begins within the aspects of mind, body, and soul. Quantum healing looks beyond the symptoms and directs itself straight to the source of the issue. Sifting through the emotional layers and years of human conditioning, expanded awareness seeks to find the root cause, face it, forgive it, and alchemize it through the power of unconditional love. Purifying, a quantum approach to well-being, brings the power of light, which is the most powerful cleanser there is.

As one comes into greater alignment with inner stillness—the unified field, the no-thingness that surrounds us—a shift takes place from a space of resistance to one of allowing. The concept of surrender begins to merge within the individual consciousness, making it possible for the spontaneous expression of universal energy to be realized as healing. The one main aspect of the unified field is desire—the desire for the potential within it to be actualized, which can be expressed as joy, happiness, inner strength, and even healing. In other words, life seeks to express itself always.

Being in alignment with stillness is a surrendered state of awareness, and because of its high-frequency energy, it clears the energetic roadblocks that prevent spontaneous healing. Everything is consciousness, and when it comes to mind, body, and soul, consciousness always seeks to be in balance, and inner stillness is the balanced state. Everything is always speaking to us—our physical bodies, our emotions, our well-being, or lack thereof. Tuning in to the body's wisdom, acknowledging our emotions and recognizing what they're trying to tell us, and paying attention to how we feel is self-empowering and expands our awareness.

Through this greater awareness, we come closer to understanding the nature of consciousness and the potential within it, as stillness speaks to us. As one anchors their awareness more and more in the present moment, time, in a sense, is no longer a consequence. The understanding is that a life can be healed on all levels in one instant through surrender and letting go; that is the power and potential that is within us, within the unified field of consciousness. Transcendent in every way, pure awareness—inner stillness is what I'm talking about—doesn't stop to contemplate how long one has endured a particular condition because only the one moment is acknowledged in the spiritual realm.

The field of unconditional love, the quantum reality's effects, are always maximal. Love is always being expressed from the field because that's what it is. Let's now look at three insights that will help shift you into greater alignment and awareness of the spontaneous and healing nature of the unified field, the dimension of inner stillness:

- Fear fends off spontaneous healing. It's the shadow self, the egoic aspect of us that blankets our awareness of the field of potential and possibility.

- Desire and intention can shift reality. It's the doorway to making change within ourselves and the world around us.

- The closer one is in alignment with their inner being, the closer one is to experiencing the soul's spontaneous nature. And the now moment is the key to this realization.

The soul, our very minds, are our connection to the unified field and its spontaneous healing potential. Moving past self-limiting beliefs and facing our fears make room for the soul to come to our awareness. And this gives the highest self the potential to express through us as the miracle of healing on the quantum levels of mind and spirit, which is then reflected in the physical.

Clearing Energy Blocks

Before we look into the restorative and energy-healing power of being one with the highest self, we're going to have a brief look at the cause of universal energy disruption between us and Source. A clear picture is needed to reveal what separation does to our energetic field, and how it spills into other aspects of our lives. When we operate primarily through the egoic, or conditioned mind, we create energetic barriers between ourselves and Source Energy.

Universal energy is always flowing to us and through us—unconditionally—but it's mainly fear (which is in essence the ego) that blocks that energy from fully extending to us. As a result of that energy blockage, one could experience the feeling of being less grounded, or find it difficult to express themselves in relationships, for example.

When we allow these energy blockages to go unchecked, they tend to accumulate or layer upon each other, making the fear seem more real. Here is one thing to be mindful of with regard to fear: it was never intended to keep one stuck energetically, but rather be the catalyst to awakening. These energetic blocks we experience as human beings serve a purpose. They are to show those who become aware of them what's not working. These energy blocks speak to us and essentially beg us to acknowledge and face them, forgive if necessary, and release them as to welcome back inner balance.

Fear, at one point or another, has created roadblocks in our lives; the fear of failure, the fear of loss, the fear of abandonment, even the fear of change and success. These all begin with energy, and the solution is one that is spiritual in nature. Becoming aware and identifying the fear is the starting point to greater self-awareness, as it puts us more in tune with our physical bodies and the energy within and surrounding us. Not having that conscious connection with our authentic self, our spiritual nature, is what allows fear to affect us energetically. Separation, the belief that we're separate from the highest self, and not knowing the truth of who we are in Source are what gives us that feeling of being on this journey alone. But nothing could be further from the truth.

Separation is an illusion. As spiritual beings having a human experience, we've been conditioned to believe that Source is outside of us. But here's the thing: Source is All That Is. Source becomes what Source creates. It's only a lack of awareness that closes us off from the direct experience of who we really are. Oneness, which represents our spiritual reality, is that which heals us energetically, activating and lighting up our chakras and healing the belief in separation. In the light of consciousness, the darkness is revealed as illusory in nature, allowing for it to be consumed in the present moment, in the presence of unconditional love.

Oneness begins with awareness. Understandably, the idea that you are one with Source may seem impossible initially, but quiet meditation, going within, and tuning in to the stillness that is already present in all of us reveals the reality of it. In other words, a spiritual teacher can point you inward and offer you insights, but the experience of oneness is a direct and personal experience.

The healing potential in oneness is almost beyond words. Clearing up our energetic fields and healing us from within, the power of oneness can then extend to our outer world. Unlike the limiting nature of separation, oneness is unlimited in what it can produce within and without. As a direct experience with Source Energy, oneness is renewing. It's the space of awareness where you find your authentic self and the healing, guidance, and spiritual tools necessary to make your life a success.

Living from the Inside-Out

This is a very important topic of discussion, as living from the inside-out (rather than from the outside-in) enables us to observe the world around us through awareness and surrender to what is rather than react to it through the egoic mind, which works tirelessly at painting not only ourselves but others and the outer world, according to its limiting perspective. Our choices, as we navigate life, are as follows: to allow the outer world to determine our state of being, which leaves us feeling disempowered and uncertain as our vital energy is displaced, or to choose to operate from a centered space, one of mind, body, soul alignment, where we look at ourselves and what appears outside of us through the surrendered state of stillness (oneness).

We already know, through experience, what operating from the outside-in does to us mentally and emotionally; as we've all experienced suffering, on some level, that comes from this mode of operation. Our focus here will be on what living from the inside-out looks like as a surrendered state and discovering the ways to return to this space of awareness as you go about your day, which will not only be calming but also renewing, thereby giving you the strength to face challenges with greater assurance.

Keep in mind that there's great strength in surrender. Making the decision to not fight against or resist a circumstance, a particular thing in the outer world, or a current health condition restores your inner peace and allows you to lay your defenses aside, shifting you into a more relaxed state. It's this relaxed state, backed by faith in the highest self combined with trusting the process even when you can't see the next step to take just yet that makes anything and all things possible, including spontaneous healing. In this space of awareness, one doesn't focus upon, repeat in their minds, nor complain about an undesirable circumstance, which includes a health challenge. Instead, one observes the thinking mind as it attempts to make the circumstance a further reality by cementing it in one's mind.

In this state, the focus of energy and attention is placed in the moment, communing with the highest self through the awareness of inner stillness. By knowing who you are and experiencing it directly through stillness, *what really matters* comes into focus. Knowing who you are relative to Source and experiencing the peace, joy, and healing that emanate from it makes what's going on "out there" pale in comparison. It's about knowing your priorities, which is tending to one's vibrational frequency on a moment-by-moment basis because the understanding is that by doing this, embodying this, through inner awareness, the outer, or manifested, world will not only begin to reflect your inner world but will also respond to you in ways that are unimaginable.

These responses include, but are not limited to, physical healing; healed, new, and more harmonious relationships; abundance; opportunities you couldn't even think of; and synchronicities that will amaze you, leaving you feeling awe and wonder. What all this really is, is a shift in focus and attention. It's understanding that you don't attempt change in the manifested world by meeting it with resistance, negative emotion, and nonacceptance, but rather you allow change to unfold by flowing with the forward flow of universal energy that is within you, by allowing your desires to be expressed through you, and by letting the inner conflict go as you realize the futility in it.

Operating through the surrendered state, or state of flow, affords you profound clarity and insights. This way of being allows for solutions to arise amidst a dilemma or problem, often spontaneously, as one is in what I would describe as "the receiving mode." When we're stressed, feeling rushed, and tired, we not only feel uninspired but also aren't so receptive if inspiration were to present itself. In other words, operating from the inside-out aligns you with your inner being, the silent witness, and all of the clarity that it is. In this frame of mind, one is no longer distracted by the outer world, but puts it in its rightful place as one's inner being and the gifts that come from embodying it are brought forward and allowed to express in order to truly live a successful life, starting from within.

Five Ways to Align with Living Inside-Out

I now offer five ways to live from a more inside-out mode of operation, which will empower you to cultivate greater clarity, focus, and awareness. The upside to this way of being is that it automatically raises your vibrational frequency. By doing so, you become more open to being aware of and receiving inspiration and insights from the higher mind.

- Cultivate being mindful and resonating with the present moment. Doing so will bring your awareness more in alignment with spirit.

- Observe your inner world of thought and emotion, and make it a practice. The more you can create space and observe the thinking mind, the greater your awareness and sense of personal freedom will arise.

- Remember that the outer world is only a projection of your inner world. Being mindful that it's a mirror will hone your ability to discern.

- Don't take things or life too seriously. Life really should be joyful, harmonious, and blissful. We have to remember gentleness and softness, with ourselves and in how we treat others.

- Remember that the inner and outer worlds are spiritual in nature, and to see them clearly, one must do so through inner stillness, a silent or quieted mind. The realization that inner stillness is a reality is where one starts with bringing this reality to life.

Soul and Miracle Awareness

Not only is the soul spontaneous by nature, but so are the miracles that express through soul awareness. The soul—being an individualized aspect of Source—has all the same potential, attributes, and capabilities of the highest self. With that comes the experience of miracles through the surrendered state of spirit.

Miracles are quite natural in the spiritual realm, including this reality. It's our human conditioning—being convinced that we're closed off or separate from the divine and all the potential within it, *potential* meaning "power," as it's translated from Latin—that limits the spontaneity of the soul and the miracles it produces effortlessly and naturally. We're going to look deeper into this characteristic and how you can embody it more, allowing for the possibility of miracles to express in your life and remind you of who and where you really are.

When you operate through soul awareness, the realization that comes through that awareness is that everything is a miracle—that the miracle is unfolding, moment by moment, as life itself. Consciousness is the source of everything, including the miracle that is the manifested world. Just think, everything in this world, the world itself, is coming from nothing—the unseen realm of spirit. It's this unseen energy, this force, that is responsible for making life possible. Being mindful of this, one is reminded to be grateful for this gift called life.

The soul (being pure consciousness itself), on a personal level, is responsible for the expression of the miracle that is your life and all that is found in it. When in alignment with its essence, which is stillness, one shifts into a miracle state of mind. Untethered from the limitations of the conditioned mind, one is flowing with universal energy and is one with their desires, allowing for their expression through nonresistance.

Being in a miracle state of mind, together with its spontaneity, shifts you into the realm of receiving life-altering miracles that can give you a momentary glimpse into the spiritual realm. In this receiving state, you can experience mystical events, such as visions, an audible experience with the highest self, third eye activation, and even spontaneous healing. Even experiencing a synchronicity is an example of a miracle being expressed. Because of their source, miracles are unlimited by nature and defy all laws of this world. These events are always spontaneous, taking place when they're least expected. Cultivating awareness of inner stillness, and the potential teeming within it, makes having these out-of-this-world events a possibility.

Giving up our need for control—of trying to control others or the outer world for that matter—allows the positive, forward, and desire-bringing flow of life to express to us and through us. By surrendering to the highest self, which is really inner alignment, we become one with it, as we activate potentials (dormant forces within us, such as the chakras), which can propel us, shift us in fact, into higher and more energetically aligned timelines that reflect our ever-evolving state of being.

Five Soul- and Spontaneity-Cultivating Tips

I want to wrap up this section by giving you five tips to aligning more with the soul and its spontaneity. Being mindful of these insights and concepts can be elevating, as they are expressions from another realm, shifting you toward a soul awareness—one where all things are possible.

- Cultivate awareness through meditation, reading, or exploring your passions. Awareness is the key to experience; it's what opens the door to possibility.

- Practice becoming flexible in your thinking. Be open enough to see other's perspectives and point of views—this practice is soul aligning and leads to understanding.

- Be spontaneous! Not everything has to be preplanned. Deciding to take a trip last minute or to go out with a friend on the spur of the moment, shifts you out of the conditioned mind's rigid structure.

- Listen to your gut more. The soul is spontaneous by nature, and it often uses gut feelings to get a message or inspiration across.

- Try not to predict outcomes, but rather, let go and let Source take over. Letting go and trusting is one of the most soul-affirming actions and energy you could ever put forth into the universe.

Chapter Seven
Unifying Mind, Body, and Soul

Bringing awareness back to the body, and its innate intelligence, begins with the awareness that the mind and the soul are intimately connected with your physicality—that the three are not separate from each other. From that space of clarity, one can choose to decide to take inner and outer action to connect deeper with the soul, which will automatically make you more in tune with the subtle body, what the body needs, and how it communicates with you. In this section, the subtle body guided me to emphasize the importance of reconnecting and being in tune with the body.

The subtle body, as I reflected on its innate wisdom, expressed that over time many of us have become disconnected from our bodies through human conditioning and outer distractions. This is not a judgment but an observation. For change and positive shifts to take place, the unconscious aspects of oneself have to be looked at, not ignored—this, in a sense, is the overall concept of shadow work. This insight resonated deeply with me, and I would add that not knowing there's a level of awareness beyond the thinking mind combined with identifying with it (the ego) are in fact two of humanity's greatest obstacles. They close one off from not only realizing there's more to us, to consciousness, but also from directly experiencing higher states.

Taking your attention and awareness away from the outside world and directing it inward, even for brief moments, to reflect and contemplate one's spiritual and mental aspects, not only gives life to them through awareness but also invites clarity to reveal to you that you're more than just a body—you are a three-part being. Being in touch with the soul through mindfulness connects you to the subtle body and its intelligence. Remembering that both the soul and the subtle body communicate through feelings, spontaneous insights, and energetic nudges, similar to an instant message or knowing, makes understanding them easier, allowing you to feel and tune in to divine guidance as you navigate this physical life. You become more aware and therefore more comfortable in your skin, becoming more receptive to the information coming from higher dimensions.

To clarify, what we're talking about is soul awareness in order to reconnect—the awareness of inner stillness, which is available to us all, allowing us to come into a more centered state of being. I have found that by going inward, the light and clarity of stillness reveals through inner silence that mind, body, and soul are in fact one.

Ten Ways to Reconnect Mind, Body, and Soul

The awareness of inner stillness is a very powerful way to reconnect with the body's inner intelligence. But there are also other ways to reconnect with the body. Here are ten ways to cultivate the mind-body-soul connection:

- Practicing yoga is a great way to cultivate the connection to one's body through movement and breathing.

- Set aside time every day to put away the electronics and just be. In other words, slow down and realize that the magic of life is happening now—in the moment.

- Move your body often, daily if possible. Stretch, go for a walk, dance, or exercise, as they all produce feel-good chemicals called endorphins.

- Take time to meditate. A few minutes a day of tuning in to stillness aligns you with your inner being, strengthening the mind-body-soul connection.

- Find an activity that you're passionate about. Enthusiasm is a great way to bring together doingness with beingness.

- Spend time in nature. Exposure to the natural elements contributes to your well-being and reduces stress in the process.

- Practice breathwork. Being mindful of your breathing and taking just a few minutes a day to breathe deeply, slowly, and steadily, calms the nervous system, which, when cultivated, can be helpful during times of stress.

- Practice mindfulness. Being present and aware of the now, throughout the day, raises your vibrational frequency, aligning you with the soul.

- Walk barefoot on grass. Connecting with the earth is not only grounding but also has calming effects.

- Do the necessary shadow work. Shadow work is the process of facing the dark aspects of ourselves, the negative emotions that layer over us through our human conditioning. Ways of doing shadow work include observing negative thought and responding to it rather than reacting; practicing forgiveness;

and doing exercises geared toward releasing negativity—all of which assists in clearing negative emotions and inner conflict, allowing you to embody your spiritual nature more fully.

Taking Self-Responsibility

A large part of our personal evolution journey, which is the return to wholeness, is the idea of holding oneself accountable for their own vibrational frequency and all the elements that make it up. By taking ownership for the way we feel and by understanding that our well-being (even happiness) is ultimately an inside job, we stop searching for fulfillment in the outer world, allowing us to actually enjoy what it offers, such as relationships and all of life's other experiences, without the fear of loss.

Placing the responsibility on someone else for our happiness, for example, is bound to disappoint us at some point because not everyone is a mind reader. Shifting the responsibility for our joy, peace, and happiness into our own hands, we grow and align more with the wholeness of our inner being.

Looking at self-responsibility through a wholeness-based approach, we apply it to our mind, body, and soul. Starting with the mind, we need to simply create greater awareness through self-understanding. Understanding that we're always operating with polarities—the dark and the light, the ego and the soul—we can approach the thinking mind with greater discernment and the freedom to choose differently when presented with a negative emotion or outlook.

The great thing about this process—of looking at the ego, consciously—is that it automatically begins to give you reflections from the soul and insights, offering you clarity as to your true nature. This process also, as it unfolds, breaks down the walls of separation, the thoughts that have blanketed stillness, allowing quiet to return to the mind. With a quieted mind comes even more clarity and the sense of oneness.

With the cultivation of self-responsibility comes the understanding that the physical body serves many purposes and requires regular use, through exercise and movement, as well as proper nutrition, to function optimally. Being a vessel for the divine within you that is you, the physical body, through expanded awareness, is seen as a gift and an instrument with which you can engage and interact with the manifested world. From this perspective, the body is honored for what it provides, and so, one engages in physicality, knowing it's one of the three aspects of one's beingness. I should also mention that when exercise is done with joy, with passion, and with gratitude, it allows for the fuller expression of the soul during those moments, shifting you in more alignment with your true nature, bringing closer together all three aspects of oneself.

Moving on to the soul, through self-reflection, quiet contemplation, and meditation, you can tune in to your inner being and allow its clarity and insights to be expressed as inspiration and even revelation. We often hear that life is a gift, and it is. Because of that, we have an opportunity to give back, not only by sharing our talents or by being of service but also by evolving to fulfill our highest potential through self-realization. For it's in our self-discovery process that we offer the greatest gift back to Source—realizing and knowing who you are, relative to Source itself. This is your soul purpose and, beyond anything you'll ever accomplish in the outside world, coming into soul awareness will be your greatest success and achievement.

The interesting thing surrounding this spiritual kind of success is that once you're self-realized, through inner stillness, you open the door to making your dreams and desires come to fruition. The reasoning behind this is that resistance and inner conflict has been laid aside. You're now flowing with and drinking from the eternal fountain of life; one that is always guiding, continually renewing, and constantly allowing you to be re-born, moment by moment. In taking personal accountability for your life, starting with the mind, you are led by divine guidance and forces *that are for you*, which have one motivation: to lead you back to soul awareness and the completeness that is your inner being.

A Self-Empowered State

Operating as one, through the awareness of inner stillness, elevates every experience and transforms even mundane tasks, as one is in direct communion with the highest self. What transpires as you go about doing whatever it is that you're doing is that your inner being is allowed to shine through as you embody your spiritual nature. The ego is no longer the dominant presence in your mind, and instead, the highest self and its wisdom, clarity, understanding, and strength are now front and center to your awareness. Being and feeling more of your authentic, spiritual self, you're no longer distracted by what has passed nor concerned over the future, as you're aware it's being called forth through the present moment. Operating through oneness is a high-vibrational state of being, and the state of enlightenment, the dimension of inner stillness, is experienced as a focused and alert, yet calm, mind.

We need to demystify the state of enlightenment in order for you to realize it's not only a possibility in your lifetime but is actually your fifth-dimensional version, already present within you as your inner being. You really don't become enlightened but instead realize enlightenment by remembering or rejoining consciously with the highest self. In this state, the egoic, thinking mind is dissolved, having lost its grip on your consciousness. It only appears occasionally throughout the day, now serving as contrast to your light, as preference—when making a choice—but ultimately, it becomes a reminder to come back to the present moment and the safety of your inner being.

The most powerful state you can embody (the state of oneness) is a merging of the local and higher mind, allowing for profound clarity and spiritual guidance as you navigate daily life. In a balanced experience, there's always a certain degree of ebb and flow in the awareness of stillness. Sometimes it is more like a soft melody in the background, and at other times, it is more apparent to your conscious mind.

Having returned to wholeness, you're now not only empowered to live with greater confidence and certainty but you're also fully equipped to be of service to others, reminding them through your demonstration of who they are and what their potential is. Like a candle being lit in the darkness, you, through spiritual embodiment, become a way-shower, pointing others inward toward their own light of consciousness. After all, this is ultimately what we're all up to on one level or another: to be of service to others. Some souls have come to offer you the gift of contrast, through varying degrees of awareness. Other souls have come into your life to remind you of lessons, perhaps in forgiveness and nonattachment. Through the clarity of enlightenment, this empowered state reveals to you that everything and everyone is a teacher, offering you a reminder in some form.

When you are no longer reacting to the outside world, or if you do, any perceived trespass is quickly alchemized in the light of stillness, you are reminded by the higher mind of what's real and what is not. You see harmony and flow and recognize synchronicity when you observe the outer world as now being an extension of your consciousness.

Everything now speaks to you energetically; you're able to pick up on the subtle, deeper meanings behind the message, such as a billboard on the side of a bus, a conversation with a friend, or the message in a fortune cookie. Functioning as one, the infinite intelligence within you (as your soul, subtle body, and higher mind) now works in concert—you're operating beyond thought. Guided by the higher dimensional information that is teeming within the light of stillness, that intelligence is now flowing through each chakra, cell, organ, and bodily system, because one has become fearless—having cast out any and all darkness.

This self-empowered version of you already exists in the unseen, spiritual realm. Being an extension of Source itself and a part of the will of Source, the soul will not yield to this world nor its trappings. Unmoved, unshaken, and unafraid, the stillness of your inner being is not only your guiding compass inward but because of what it is—unconditional love—it will not reduce itself to meet you halfway. Because love is ever-expanding by nature, it is us who are called to rise in consciousness, to awaken to the reality of inner stillness and its essence, which is love in its purest representation—without condition nor limits.

The Circle Is Complete

Realizing that there's a level of awareness beyond the thinking mind and experiencing self-actualization by awakening to the dimension of inner stillness, you soon realize that every aspect of you is creative and expressive by nature. Through the recognition of your spiritual nature, you understand the roles that the mind, body, and soul all have in the creative or manifesting process. Your soul, being one with Source, is your direct line to your desires and inspiration.

A quick sidebar: Source seeks to experience itself, and life, through you because you are, in fact, all one—nothing is separate in the unseen world of spirit. Source is life and is you, while also experiencing itself as countless other manifestations. Now that we've gotten that out of the way, back to the soul.

Your dreams and aspirations are sponsored by the highest self. These images, visions, and dreams for your life are there for a purpose: for you to actualize them and bring them to life. Understandably, some dreams can seem so big that they may seem out of reach. But when you realize who's sponsoring your dreams; who you are; and what's possible through faith, trust, and surrender, what once seemed impossible now becomes not only possible but probable.

With inspiration and your dreams presented to you, the next part of completing the circle is to harness the power of one's mind through intention, focus, and direction. You have the ability to imagine for a reason: to plant your desires deep into the fertile ground of your consciousness, into stillness, as you water them with gratitude and appreciation. Using the practice of nonattachment, you tend to the weeds of doubt, fear, and uncertainty consciously by seeing them for what they are: illusions sponsored by the ego. In that process, you remember to let go of how and when the desire will come to fruition, trusting in the universe's divine timing. Following your dreams with your mind, you take the necessary action to merge the fifth-dimensional dream to the manifested world. Following your passion and being of service in the process is a powerful combination in making one's dreams come true.

In taking positive, dream-fulfilling action now and embodying who you are spiritually by choosing happiness and gratitude and cultivating unconditional love now, you make the mind, body, and soul circle complete—this is the manifesting process, in essence.

The soul inspires, the mind creates, and the physical body experiences. We are meant to be active participants in life, not sit on the sidelines. The key is remembering who you are and reclaiming the immense power found in oneness—your interconnectedness with everything and everyone, seen and unseen, as to remember that all of life is for you.

Moving Forward with Direction

There are many different, effective approaches that can be taken to help us create a greater sense of well-being and oneness. Looking at health and healing through the lens of wholeness includes a mind, body, and soul approach. Acknowledging all three of these aspects and integrating them in our actions toward inner balance can lead to tremendous results. Going inward and asking the following questions can create an atmosphere where one is led to answers: What does my mind need? What does my body need? What does my soul need?

Beginning this process of asking and tuning in to the wisdom within invites greater awareness into the picture. It can assist in clearing up confusion as to where to start and guide us as to which direction to take. Each action taken adds a piece to the puzzle of wholeness, making things clearer. In other words, there are no small actions when they are taken with intention and on a conscious level; it all adds to complete the bigger picture.

Each aspect of our being calls us to be aware of something. It may slightly differ for each of us, but you will probably note some general commonalities.

Mind: Relaxation, calmness, direction, focus, and centeredness

Body: Nutrition, movement, balanced eating, appreciation, and rest

Soul: Awareness, expression, alignment, stillness, and inspiration

Looking at the mind, it calls us to shift from a busy and perhaps intense state to one of relaxation and centeredness. It also requires our conscious direction so that we can manifest our reality on a conscious level. Having focus allows us to create a vision for ourselves and our lives. In other words, the mind requires our conscious engagement, calling us to be active participants in the manifestation process.

Being the converter of energy, the body requires a nutrient-filled diet to function optimally. Because of different body types, it's best to find out what works for you through trial and error, or perhaps through a holistic nutritionist. Moving the body routinely and paying attention when rest is needed are great ways to release energy and also improve sleep. Having a balanced diet not only has us feeling good but also provides the necessary vitamins and minerals to support overall health. Having an appreciation for the body, in its healing capability, positively impacts our cells; our cells raise in frequency when love is extended to them.

The soul desires for you to be aware of it! Self-awareness. In being self-aware, you can consciously align with the soul, experience the healing of inner stillness, and feel the inspiration that flows from it. The soul, being Source itself, seeks to know itself while being with the body. It desires to express itself, and when we shift into alignment with it, we release universal energy, allowing for the potential of energetic healing to become a possibility in our reality. That healing has the potential to extend and positively impact virtually all areas of our lives.

Meditation is a great way to unify mind, body, and soul on a conscious level. Being in the moment, observing one's breaths, and just being thins the walls that separate our aspects and reminds us that each of us is a reflection of each other. Calming to the mind, restoring to the body, and soul-aligning, meditation has a soothing effect.

As the thinking mind is observed, stillness, (presence) is invited to the forefront of our awareness. It's within that vibrational frequency where wholeness is realized that you connect with the highest self.

Inner balance is an ongoing, life-long process between negativity and positivity, the unconscious and conscious, the dreamer and the awakened within. Coming into this world, the negativity, the unconscious, the dreamer is what is offered. It's up to us to consciously choose positivity and a conscious approach through the awakened state to live a balanced life.

⑥ Oneness Chanting Guided Meditation ⑥

I want to close this chapter off with a short but powerful guided meditation designed to remind you of your oneness in mind, body, soul, and beyond. This chanting meditation will assist in directing you deeper toward the oneness of your inner being: pure consciousness. This particular meditation only takes five to eight minutes, and it can be practiced once or twice weekly.

Ideally, get into a space free of distractions. You can sit or lie down for this, as long as you're comfortable.

Once you're in position, take a few deep breaths to become centered, as your breaths remind you to be present, in the now. Drop your shoulders.

As you're relaxing into the moment, take a few more deep breaths and let go of any resistance within you. If thoughts arise, observe them, remembering not to be afraid.

When you're relaxed and ready, repeat the following chant three times, with knowing, slowly, and with gentle confidence: "I am one in mind, body, and soul.

I am one with Source. I am whole and complete. I recognize my oneness with others and all of life."

Once you're done chanting, take three to four minutes to reflect on what you've just chanted. Feel the oneness of your inner being. Feel your oneness with your immediate surroundings. If you feel inspired, offer gratitude for the reality of oneness and for the moment you're experiencing.

Once you're done reflecting, take a few deep breaths and open your eyes. Bring your awareness back to the present and to your surroundings. Allow the reality of your oneness to remind you always that you're never alone, but always divinely guided, supported, and unconditionally loved.

Chapter Eight
The Field of Healing and Miracles

When activated, the doorway to the dimension of inner stillness—the third eye—sets off a chain of spiritual reactions that activates all other chakras, illuminating one from within. The third eye is a powerful spiritual faculty within us all that has not only been overlooked but also misunderstood. My desire in this chapter is to shed light on the sixth chakra and explain how it's always operating at some level and how its activation can empower you in virtually every facet of your life. I'll then end with an intention focusing on third eye activation, as this powerful awakening event cannot be forced but welcomed with desire.

Third eye activation is an instant, spontaneous awakening, taking place in the "twinkling of an eye" that is sparked by a combination of suffering, desire, and surrender. When the third eye opens, it awakens you from the dreaming state of thought, bringing your awareness toward the unchanging and eternal reality of inner stillness—your true mind. Stepping consciously into stillness, you realize your spiritual nature and shift from belief to knowing, from spiritual concepts and theory to embodying the soul through a quieted mind. The shift to knowing through spiritual embodiment takes place as the ego is cast out, and what remains is pure awareness—awareness of Source Energy and all of its wisdom, clarity, and understanding.

Raising your vibrational frequency to that of stillness (that clear and high frequency state of awareness) allows the subtle body to come online fully, as every chakra is healed, activated, and opened. A light-filled state, your conscious mind now identifies with the mind of Source. In this expanded awareness, mind, body, and soul are remembered to be one, and the light of the soul is allowed to shine through every level of your being, including the subtle body. You literally become light-filled.

It's important to mention that the third eye is always at play, on some level. One's level of spiritual awareness determines just how aware one is to the synchronicities and spiritual messages that are always being offered. A good gauge to just how much would be one's level of intuition—the ability to discern and know when one is being divinely guided.

The third eye has tremendous potential because its activation leads you to the miracle state of inner stillness, where all things become possible, including things such as emotional and spontaneous healing. With the shift from separation to oneness, your inner world shifts toward the reality of spirit, which is then reflected outward. This change in perception results in clarity, as you come to understand yourself and others, which can elevate your relationships and the world around you in a very positive and profound way. Because you're embodying the soul in this elevated awareness, you're able to tap into strength, courage, and fearlessness, which allows you to live more confidently and empowered. Third eye activation involves the integration of cosmic energies, and it is also described as kundalini awakening.

Third Eye Activation Intention

The third eye activation intention is for those who are ready to shift beyond the thinking mind and come into the dimension of inner stillness. The key elements for inviting third eye activation are desire and a spirit of surrender, in wanting to let go and allow your highest self to divinely guide you in all of life's matters. From my personal experience, a one-time intention is all that's needed, as you let go of how and when.

The intention, which will be directed to the highest self, should preferably be spoken, as there's more energy behind words than thoughts alone. To set the intention, say: "I am aware of the third eye and its potential. I am ready to shift beyond the thinking mind and come into stillness. I am surrendering myself to the power and potential within me, and I am surrendering the timing of this event to the highest self."

Kundalini Awakening

With so much emphasis on the subtle body throughout this book, I felt it important to include the topic of kundalini and kundalini awakening. Having undergone this experience as a spontaneous awakening through third eye activation, I have deep insights into the potential and power of this cosmic energy.

The kundalini is a dormant, life-changing force that is within everyone. When brought to life, this energy has the power to consume any darkness, as it's based in unconditional love that is ushering in healing, which is a return to wholeness. Translated from Sanskrit, *kundalini* translates as "coiled snake." The coiled snake is resting dormant at the base of the spine, but when awakened it rises, activating all chakras and filling one's body with light and unrestricted cosmic energy.

Kundalini awakening cannot be forced, but there are practices that one can do to shift closer to one's spiritual self, making the potential for this type of awakening a possibility. The cosmic energy that is kundalini is based out of the dimension of inner stillness, also known as universal or cosmic consciousness. By transcending the limits of the egoic, or thinking mind, kundalini awakening is total illumination of one's mind, revealing the dark and the light, simultaneously. This is what is described as the thinning of the veil from within, revealing the true nature of the manifested world, which is spiritual.

An extension of your higher consciousness, or mind, this energy is a major source of inner power, strength, vitality, and intelligence. The chakras are the transformers, and when fully activated through awakening, they take this high-powered, cosmic energy and convert it to light-filled information, allowing one to embody clarity, wisdom, and understanding. The potential found in this kind of awakening includes spontaneous healing on all levels—mind, body, and soul—the coming online of psychic abilities, as well as the ability to access higher dimensions of consciousness.

Five Ways to Activate Kundalini Energy

Now that we've looked at the potential of kundalini, let's look at ways to raise, activate, and align with it consciously, as I find it is important to offer insights into your potential as well as ways to make the information applicable so you can begin to resonate and embody these spiritual concepts.

- Because of its connection with the third eye, the practice of challenging negative thinking aligns one closer and inward, toward one's inner being and the energy emanating from inner stillness.

- Meditation upon the present moment and the dimension of inner stillness raises one's vibrational frequency, shifting one's energy to match that of kundalini.

- Relaxation techniques, such as listening to high-frequency music, brings you into greater alignment with your spiritual self.

- Practicing a positive outlook serves you by elevating your mood and allowing you to practice gratitude and appreciation, both of which are based in unconditional love.

- Cultivating mindfulness and the spiritual forces of faith, trust, and surrender shifts one closer to the miracle state of stillness, where all things become possible, including spontaneous awakening, the moment one realizes its reality.

The Miracle State

With focus on the dimension of inner stillness in this chapter, we need to recognize the fact that stillness is the often overlooked and unrecognized dimension of clarity and peace within, as it's based in oneness with Source. Manifested reality—the world of form—is where we come to forget who and where we are, as we become hypnotized by the thinking mind and the separate-appearing outer world.

This collective hypnosis has been demonstrated by the countless generations who've come before us, having not awakened. There is, however, perfection in that. Timing is everything, and the ego in previous generations hadn't reached peak levels of fear, confusion, and, in a sense, insanity, until this generation. Despite how bleak or dark the world currently seems, we're at a point in our history where things are actually incredibly exciting, as the potential for a collective awakening has not only become a possibility but a certainty, especially if we're to survive, evolve, and grow.

I'll attempt to use words, which are forms, to describe formlessness, the state of inner stillness. A picture will begin to take shape when one awakens to the dimension of inner stillness and begins to identify and align with this transcendent state, rather than identifying with the thinking mind. It is not only a life-changing inner experience; stillness has the potential to shift you into a new, more desirable reality, or higher timeline.

The spiritual realm is described as the miracle state because inner stillness is the quantum, or unified field. It's within every cell of your body, and it is found within everything and everyone. It is in fact, all-encompassing, as it's the mind of Source.

The birthplace for miracles, potential, and every possible experience, stillness is that undifferentiated field that can become anything, as it is no-thing. Stillness is limitless in every way because it's beyond the limitations and restrictions of the egoic mind, so consciously becoming one with stillness makes all things possible.

The direct experience of inner stillness is had through a silent mind, which is reflective of the mind of Source. A state free of inner conflict, stillness is the unification of your will with the will of Source. What Source wills for you is to be empowered through the clarity of stillness (wholeness), which is experienced as wisdom, understanding, and inner peace—and that's just the start. What was once thought of as being separate from you is now known and experienced directly through the silence of your inner being. Through stillness, one experiences the peace that is forever being reflected from it. Unconditional love, bliss, joy, and authenticity become one's core vibrational frequency through this state because that's what your inner being is.

You're still able to experience the egoic, thinking mind, but you no longer identify with it because the truth of stillness, of who you are, has been revealed. Through inner stillness awareness, the ego loses its bite and is no longer a source of one's suffering, but becomes contrast to your inner light and a reminder to come back to the now, to stillness, when it presents itself through projection.

The great thing about operating through this centered state of being is that you no longer hold on to negative, limiting emotions that may have, at one point in time, kept you stuck in those lower vibrations for days, weeks, months, or years. The transmutation of negativity now takes place instantly, as one is awake to their inner power and to the negative effects of energizing and identifying with negative emotions. Living masterfully, moment by moment, one lets go of the last moment to step into a new one, a new reality, with all of its potential.

Being divinely guided by the higher mind and soul, you're able to bring to life and develop latent spiritual faculties, such as psychic abilities and the mountain-moving forces of faith, trust, and surrender. These spiritual gifts can come to the forefront of one's consciousness along with clarity, wisdom, and understanding because there's no longer anything distracting you or suppressing them. Negative emotions have been dissolved by the all-consuming fire that is stillness, which burns up anything unlike unconditional love. Fear can't operate or last long in the presence of this love, as it's pure, light-filled, and unchanging.

I can attest that being aware of and in alignment with inner stillness makes spontaneous healing a possibility. As you realize that healing has taken place at the level of mind, which is the shift from separation (the thinking mind) to oneness (inner stillness), that healing then is reflected in the physical body, sooner or later. Free of the idea of separation, the soul is resurrected and rises to your awareness, allowing its power and strength to fully activate the chakras, filling you with light. Able to spin and operate optimally, the chakras and their innate wisdom begin to express themselves as feelings of being grounded, playful, powerful, compassionate, expressive, intuitive, and connected with everything in this world and beyond.

This is just a glimpse into the potential of operating consciously through the dimension of inner stillness. Having realized that enlightenment is only the beginning—living through and embodying your spiritual nature is an ever-continuous and wondrous process of evolution and becoming. Knowing there's no limits to Source, as one steps into a new reality and a new awareness, there's an understanding that there's always more waiting for you.

Zero-Point Consciousness: The Zone

Many of us have probably heard of professional athletes performing exceptionally well when they're "in the zone." This is a state where one is absolutely focused, and the athletes who shift into this state are flowing and connected with their higher minds, whether they realize it or not. In these moments, abilities are heightened, including psychic abilities such as clairvoyance, which is the spiritual faculty of being able to perceive things or people or future probabilities through extrasensory perception. In other words, those who tap in to stillness during athletics, or any other endeavor, experience a more perceptive and, in a sense, supernatural version of themselves.

Inner stillness is zero-point consciousness. It's the experience of the local mind, or awareness, merging with the no-thingness of pure consciousness—the mind of Source. Contained within the zero point, or unified field, is every possibility. Focusing on an outcome and becoming one with the desire activates within you dormant forces that bring that quantum idea, or potential, to life. The key to peak performance is the alignment with inner stillness that invokes the higher mind, allowing it to express itself as you move and operate as one—in mind, body, and soul.

When performing from zero-point consciousness, you are centered in your being and in that spiritual sweet spot—"the zone" where mental and physical abilities are enhanced. Fear is put in its place as one embodies their potential. Inner stillness is unlimited in what this level of consciousness can achieve and actualize. It is the undifferentiated field that can become and produce anything through intention, focus, visualization, and becoming one with the desired goal. Operating beyond the laws of the natural world, being in alignment with inner stillness connects you with your supernatural nature and all of its potential.

Reconnecting with Youthfulness

There's a secret that only enlightened masters were aware of, up until now. It's the secret to not only looking young but also feeling vibrant, having lots of energy, being lighthearted, personifying youthfulness, and just downright being attractive. The secret is living through your spiritual nature—the timeless dimension of inner stillness.

This may sound too good to be true, but rest assured, it's an actualized reality through the renewing state of pure consciousness. Because things such as stress and worry are things of the past when one embodies inner stillness, one shifts energetically—representing the fifth-dimensional version of themselves. Having dissolved old, tired, and limited thinking, one renews themselves in spirit, and does so on a moment-by-moment basis.

Living through spirit, you connect fully with universal, or cosmic, energy, as it fills you with light and life. This energy, being high vibrating, raises your vibrational frequency, making it impossible for lower, denser energies to cling to your energy field, restoring your vital energy. The light of consciousness shines through the eyes of these beings who know and embody inner stillness.

Over-flowing with cosmic energy through free-flowing chakras, energy abounds in this state of awareness. Being guided by inner stillness reminds one of the futility in resistance—to things or circumstances. When one allows vital energy to fill every cell, as one no longer tries to swim against the current of life, they're able to draw upon the continuous wellspring as needed, simply by surrendering, or calling it forth through intention.

Living consciously through stillness has you seeing life through a clear, light-filled lens. You're not as serious as you used to be because you've realized that the manifested world is a dream that can be shaped according to your desires and intentions. Able to laugh at yourself, you're no longer sweating the small stuff because you can see the bigger picture.

In embodying stillness, you, in essence, become one with the soul's eternal youthfulness—from a chronological standpoint, it's around the age of thirty-three. Through expanded awareness, you understand the creative power of your thoughts, words, and vibrational frequency, and because of that you don't entertain energies that are limiting and old in nature. You look young because you are young energetically, literally experiencing what you've become.

In being your spiritual, authentic self, you naturally become attractive because authenticity is desirable. Being genuine, you instill a sense of honesty, openness, and trust—qualities that others look for. Spiritually attractive people radiate love and are magnetic, drawing the right people, opportunities, and synchronicities, all in divine timing.

The key to looking and feeling younger, inner stillness is the secret to being youthful and vibrant on every level. Because it is a transcendent state, stillness identifies with no number nor age. Always renewing and reinvigorating—*as one practices the art of nonattachment*—stillness provides not only the youthful energy to renew you but also the awareness and spiritual tools to keep you connected with its vital, endless supply that extends from unconditional love—the heart of Source.

The Language of the Subtle Body and the Soul

While we're on the topic of stillness, I feel it is important to discuss further how the language of the subtle body and the soul are more easily recognized and interpreted through this expanded state. Everything becomes extraordinarily clearer through the quiet state of inner stillness. It's within the awareness of stillness that the language of the subtle body and the soul—as feelings, vibrations, energetic nudges, instant downloads, or inner knowing, all of which make up divine guidance—becomes more apparent.

The wonderful thing about becoming clearer through inner silence is you realize you're also being communicated to through the outer world—in the conversations you have and the subtle signs and symbols you encounter, such as reoccurring angel numbers (seeing three or four repeated numbers, such as 11:11 on a clock) and synchronicities. Awareness is the key to all of this; as you become more aware within, you simultaneously become more aware without.

Being completely neutral, as an experience, the centered state of stillness highlights any movement on the surface of the mind, as well as any energies in the form of messages, positive or negative. With the enhanced discernment that's afforded by stillness, you're able to quickly tell the difference between an inspiring, divinely guided message or insight versus a lower-vibrating, fear/ego-based thought. The messages coming from the subtle body (the soul) are high-vibrating, inspiring, light-feeling, instant, and nonrepetitive, essentially. Divine guidance can also come in the form of a "no" as a gut feeling, almost a wrenching feeling in the pit of your stomach, when the soul rails against an idea you're contemplating that it knows is not for you.

With the ego, the main energy is fear, and a contracting one at that. It will feel heavy, and it can appear as the energies of worry, uncertainty, anxiety, and overall self-doubt. The questions to ask oneself, when trying to determine what kind of message is being presented, are the following: Is this feeling like fear or inspiration? Is this a contracting or expansive feeling?

If you're feeling hesitancy with regard to making a decision, such as when deciding on making a large purchase for example, go within and ask yourself: Is this a *no* because it doesn't feel like it's right for me or am I hesitant because fear and uncertainty are creeping in?

Reflect on the questions and then take a few moments, while you remain present, to allow for clarification. Take even longer, if you're still not sure what step to take.

Being mindful of how love and fear, or the soul and ego, communicate gives us clarity and a greater ability to make more empowered decisions that resonate with us. Recognizing that the soul is, for the most part, more subtle in its approach, sheds light on the ego's more aggressive, fear-based approach. The more you go within and pay attention to the cues, from both the dark and the light, the more you'll hone your ability to discern. And through the cultivation of discernment will come greater intuition and even leadership abilities, as you'll not only be able to understand and read yourself more clearly but also others and even a room, or any environment you're in.

Healing and Renewal Potentials of Stillness

Being unconditional love, in essence, stillness is not only healing and renewing but is also your natural state of being. Because stillness is your natural state, so are all the wonderful, life-changing, and uplifting effects that take place in that awareness. As humans, we've forgotten how truly powerful we are when we're operating as one through mind, body, and soul. Your true self is pure consciousness, and its desire is to express what it is—to extend more of itself.

I want to begin with a simple reminder: you all have the potential inside of you to heal, renew, and evolve to become and embody that which you've believed to be impossible to actualize: Source within. Healing from the illusion of separation, by choosing love over fear, elevates one's vibrational frequency to that of the soul and is how one lets old, negative thoughts and beliefs die, allowing for the new dreams and inspirations to come to life.

Countless human beings on Earth are currently going through a spiritual metamorphosis from the immature stage of ego to the maturity and wholeness of the soul. Many are recognizing the limitations and constraints of third-dimensional consciousness, and they are deciding to lay aside the ego and step into the field of the unknown (stillness), where the separation between one and Source Energy is healed. They are allowing healing to take place first in mind and soul, and then in body. In other words, many are going to realize that the supernatural is, in fact, their natural state.

What we're talking about is the letting go of the small ideas about who we are and who Source is, relative to us humans. It's very much a shedding process, releasing the repeating and limiting cycles of linear time—the past and the future—to step into the potential of the now, and the soul, which is encountered in timelessness. This is how one dares to dream bigger; by realizing one's interconnectedness with the All That Is and allowing the flow of inspiration from the highest self to ignite your passions and dreams so they can be realized.

In my direct experience with spirit, I have realized that we are all supernatural, and it's only our sole identification with human nature that has constrained us. It's been a necessary process, but the time has come for the end of the experiment—the illusion of separation—because of how destructive the ego has become on an individual and collective level.

Reconnecting with the soul and following its lead—its divine guidance—will guide us to the healing found in oneness and the moment-by-moment renewal that's always available to us all. Keep in mind that all of this is a choice; we each have free will to keep playing with the idea of separation or to remember your reality of oneness. The very fact that one can experience the illusion of separation demonstrates that freedom to pretend to be something or someone that one is not. If that's not freedom, and unconditional love, I don't know what is.

To clarify, healing and renewal are natural effects of becoming aware of and embodying our spiritual nature. Once you become aware of the dimension of inner stillness and align with that, embody that, and operate from that, in mind and body, you allow the high-vibrating and cosmic energies of that state to flow freely through you. As the walls of separation—fear, anger, and frustration, just to name a few—dissolve in the presence of unconditional love, what remains is pure consciousness—Source Energy—and its full expression, which extends as healing, renewal, peace, joy, clarity, wisdom, understanding, discernment, strength, and so much more.

⑥ Self-Reflecting and Renewing Exercise ⑨

Building upon the information just offered, I've put together a self-reflecting and renewing exercise to assist you in cultivating awareness into your own inner potential. Always going by less is more, this exercise should only take ten to fifteen minutes, and can be practiced once a week.

You'll need a quiet area and a way to jot down some personal realizations. A pen and paper is fine, or you can use electronic means.

Take the next three to five minutes and reflect on the duality of this life experience—how we live in a world of relativity with seeming opposites. For example, you can focus on the fact that if one can think negatively, then one can think positively. If one can become angry, one can become peaceful. If one can experience fear, one can experience fearlessness. If one can experience the thinking mind with its thought forms, then one can potentially experience the silence of stillness—formlessness. And finally, if one can experience separation, dis-ease, and feeling stuck, then one, according to duality, can also experience oneness, healing, and moving forward.

Once you've contemplated on these duality concepts, come to your own conclusions regarding them.

Jot down your findings, so you can further reflect. One more thing to reflect on: Shouldn't positives be possible, if there are negatives? Reflect on this for another few minutes.

After you're done with this last reflection, take a few minutes and note any realizations that come to mind. There are really no right or wrong answers. What it all comes down to is this: You are deciding what's still serving you and what no longer does. Remember you have the freedom to always choose differently.

Your 5D Version Is Whole

As you grow spiritually, you may find that you're operating less and less from the five senses and more from feelings—reading vibrational frequency and energy—of yours and others. This is a result from aligning more with your spiritual self and less with your human conditioning. The more you become aware of and shift into higher frequencies, such as joy, appreciation, and gratitude, you may very well find that you're more sensitive to energies, subtle energies in fact. Moving closer to your unmanifested self—the soul—creates the potential and opportunity to become aware of the unified field—fifth-dimensional (5D) reality, where you're already whole and complete.

There is no "getting there" because you're already in the midst of this field. The only requirement to experiencing it, to step into it, is awareness. Doingness has nothing to do with it. There are no hills to climb, no long, arduous pilgrimage needed, but rather it has everything to do with beingness. You just have to take off the egoic mask, which is the idea of having to be defensive, and be yourself.

You have only to remember: bring awareness to the reality of the soul to reconnect to the essence of your being. Silent meditation, or self-reflection, is an excellent way to do so—just breathing and being. This allows you to become mindful of the dark, where you can recognize it, face it, forgive it, release it, and look past it while becoming more conscious of your very own inner being.

Let's look a little closer at what the experience of operating from 5D (the dimension of inner stillness) is like, and then shift to some simple insights that will assist in guiding you inward toward direct experience. The experience is one of moment-by-moment living. You are no longer operating through linear time, but you are keenly aware of the eternal moment of now and the parallel realities available to you through the unified field. The majority of your experience, approximately 95 percent, is now the direct experience of stillness, which is profoundly peaceful, healing, and renewing.

You're still able to experience the thinking mind; however, you're no longer attached to it. You are now free. Universal energy flows to you and through you, unrestricted. Inspiration is spontaneous, creativity is enhanced, and spiritual guidance is readily recognized through the developed spiritual faculty of discernment. Having realized the value of forgiveness, you are free of the past and call forth your future consciously through the present, via intention, gratitude, trust, and surrender. You now operate primarily from the soul and the higher mind. Feeling your environment energetically, you're able to recognize the one essence animating all of life. It is essentially an experience of oneness with everything, everyone, and All That Is. This is a more balanced approach to living, as you embody more of your true self while navigating life as a human being.

Five Awareness-Expanding 5D Reality Insights

Offered now are five insights that will expand your awareness of 5D reality:

- The here and now offers tremendous potential. Awareness of it raises your energetic field while also being the doorway into 5D reality, or the unified field.

- Awareness is key. What you become aware of is what creates the possibility of experience.

- The dimension of inner stillness, or 5D reality, is at the center of your core—it's your true mind, which is unchanging relative to the ever-changing nature of the ego.

- Spend time with like-minded people. Higher-vibrating beings coming together to share insights can be transforming and elevating.

- A gratitude mindset will shift you past lower, denser energies, inviting higher energies, as well as experiences, to be grateful for.

Effort is not required to directly experience the 5D mind, but rather you have to surrender. When one lets go of limiting beliefs, of what was once thought of as impossible, they shift into the potentials and possibilities of 5D reality. Tuning in to the subtle nature of spirit, we become aware of its all-encompassing presence, as awareness reminds us that there's really nowhere to go but within to experience this expanded state of consciousness.

Mental and Emotional Stability

The stabilizing factor, the most important thing to be aware of in order to bring balance and stability to our minds, is the present moment. The now is the rock in which you can lay the foundation for your mind. It is steady, faithful, consistent, unchanging, and where the peace of inner stillness can be experienced. Too much of the past creates excess sadness and depression, while too much future causes too much uncertainty and anxiety. The balance to these mind constructs is to be centered in the eternal moment of now, which brings clarity to confusion and light to the dark through spiritual alignment.

Through present-moment awareness, you shift into calmer awareness—the stability of stillness. A reflection of your authentic self, stillness is rock solid, unmoved by the waves of emotion on the surface of the mind. Being what you are, at your core— stillness that is brought to the forefront of one's consciousness— transmutes negative emotions because its essence is unconditional love. Reconnecting with the love of stillness brings your awareness back to the wholeness of your being, balancing the negative, dark aspects of the ego with the positive, light-filled aspects of your inner being. Keep in mind that the ego is a temporary identity that you took on to forget who you are eternally—spirit.

Six Ways to Cultivate Mental and Emotional Stability

There are some important insights that haven't been mentioned yet that will add to your cultivation of mental and emotional stability, as well as bring your awareness closer toward wholeness. It would be prudent to reflect on these insights often. If something doesn't resonate just yet, that's more than okay; disregard it. You can always come back to a concept and re-examine it. Here are the insights and ways to cultivate further mental and emotional stability:

- Become comfortable amidst uncomfortable feelings. This is vital to not only understand but also to put into practice. When we're experiencing heavy emotions and emotional turmoil, understandably, it can be easy to react and lose ourselves in the emotions, even try to avoid them. But if you can practice being still and centered during the ego's outbursts, it will not only further cultivate your awareness but also stabilize your mind during the storm. Being non-reactive to fear, or any other negative emotion, is what starves them, taking away their power, as you reclaim yours.

- Being vulnerable is a demonstration of strength. It sounds like a contradiction, but when we become more comfortable in sharing our emotions and some of the challenges we've faced, that's a demonstration that we're becoming more comfortable in our skin, growing and maturing spiritually. Be mindful that the adversities we face are a testimony to our strength, not weakness. In sharing our stories of adversity and triumph, we serve as a beacon of light and a source of inspiration for others.

- Balance work with play. We all have a playful side, and it's important to cultivate it, as it shifts us energetically. Having hobbies, spending time in nature, and connecting with others are great ways to lighten up and enjoy life. Not only relaxing but also having things to look forward to—things that we really enjoy, outside of work—also gives us another outlet for expression.

- See adversity as an opportunity to grow. When challenges come up in life, the conditioned response is to react and complain. Having this outlook cements the circumstance in our minds, calling forth further negative emotions. Choosing to see circumstances as neutral, or as an opportunity to grow, changes you internally, which will positively shift your outer reality. In other words, your outlook is everything, and it begins within.

- Cultivate positive feelings proactively. The daily practice of positive thinking, choosing how you want to feel intentionally, builds momentum and strengthens your mind toward the positive. In doing this, you become more well-equipped during stressful moments, allowing you to shift out of them sooner and more efficiently. Expressing (thinking and speaking) life-affirming, positive thoughts several times a day creates a positive mindset.

- Allow yourself to feel emotions. Spiritual awareness and growth, even the state of enlightenment, is not about ignoring or bypassing emotions but allowing yourself to feel them, see the messages in them, forgive if necessary, and release what doesn't serve you. Emotions are part of the human experience; the gift that comes with spiritual awareness is that you can feel the range of emotions (the dark and light) while you observe them, rather than identify with them. This approach leads to not only total liberation but also the ability to call forth emotion in order to express yourself, while knowing you are the awareness behind it all—not the emotion itself. In other words, don't be afraid to feel emotions; they cannot harm you when you know who you are—an invulnerable spiritual being having a human experience.

Ways to Embrace Wholeness Daily

From a spiritual perspective, wholeness refers to who one is spiritually already whole, complete, and equipped with everything needed to live life fully. Being whole means to be in touch with the spiritual dimension within: stillness.

Inner stillness reflects the invulnerable, eternal, and highest aspects of oneself. From this undifferentiated field of awareness, every empowering attribute and spiritual faculty springs forth, providing the knowing, insights, and tools to direct your life consciously. Keep in mind, this is not to detract from the ego, or conditioned mind, for without it, one would not be able to awaken to and fully appreciate who they are spiritually. However, the focus here will be on remembering our whole selves and ways to cultivate and embrace wholeness in our everyday lives.

Ten Ways to Cultivate and Embrace Wholeness Daily

You can embrace and cultivate wholeness through embodiment. By choosing wholeness now—living it—we experience it. In other words, there's no need to postpone embracing and expressing who you are spiritually because practical spirituality is about remembering or re-joining spirit and then acting upon that awareness. Here are ten ways to do that daily:

- Remember that you are a three-part being. It's easy to get caught up in and distracted by the thinking mind, forgetting who we really are. Taking a few minutes in your day to reflect on the fact that you're a spiritual being having a human experience will give you clarity and fresh perspective.

- Lighten up. Remembering not to take ourselves or others too seriously shifts us vibrationally, offering us relief and levity from life's everyday challenges. Being lighthearted and heart-centered brings forth compassion toward ourselves and others.

- Find your soul tribe. As you evolve and grow, you may find that you no longer resonate with some people, and that's okay. Finding a community, small or large, that supports and nourishes your growth is like food for the soul, providing you with the opportunity to share insights and gain perspective.

- Cultivate a healthy body image. This concept includes self-acceptance and self-appreciation. Extending gratitude for your physical body and for what it does for you is an example of extending self-love. Positive self-talk and being gentle with oneself and others raises your vibrational field, making you feel lighter and happier.

- Follow your dreams and passions. Our desires are inspired from the highest self. They are there for a purpose: for you to recognize them and ultimately allow them to be expressed through you so they can come to life and be experienced. This process entails mind, body, and soul working as one; it doesn't get any more whole than that.

- Believe nothing. I actually mean this literally. The goal of awakening and becoming whole is not to add anything more to you (more thoughts, more beliefs) but rather to let go of believing and come into knowing—through the quiet of stillness. In being one with the highest self, one no longer believes but observes, witnesses, and simply knows. The shift from belief to knowing delivers you to the unified field, which includes resonance, feeling, and vibrational frequency as a means of understanding.

- Practice nonattachment. Letting things go—not placing all of your happiness in someone else's hands—not only frees you but also allows the other to breathe. Sharing one's completeness, not looking to be made complete, is the conscious approach to a relationship. In other words, make happiness an inside job.

- Remember joy and bliss often. Pausing throughout the day and reflecting on these high-vibrating feelings will put a smile on your face. Reflections and attributes of the soul, reconnecting with joy and bliss, will elevate your mood and just make you feel good.

- Listen to your intuition. We all have a sixth sense, and it's based out of the sixth chakra, or third eye. Our intuition mostly speaks to us softly, often coming as a gut feeling. It can also be experienced as something more energetically pronounced, when your soul is saying "no, this is not for you" as it rails against an idea. Being in touch with your intuition and cultivating it not only aligns you closer with your inner being but can, over time, pay you dividends in saved grief and vital energy.

- Practice present-moment awareness. The now is the doorway to the unified field, the spiritual realm, where your spiritual nature and the highest self are encountered. Reminding yourself throughout the day that the present moment is all there ever is reawakens you from the mind constructs of past and future, centering you and renewing you, as you are renewed in spirit.

Chapter Nine
Maintaining Inner Balance

Life is a spiritual journey that's designed to provide you with experiences that lead you toward continual growth and expansion of consciousness. There will always be challenges in one form or another, but with the spiritual tools and insights provided through self-awareness, one is more than equipped to navigate them with greater confidence and fearlessness. It's important to remember that coming into balance is not a one-time event, but a moment-by-moment process of balancing negativity with positivity and meeting our unconscious aspect, the ego, with our awakened self through awareness of stillness.

The practice of self-awareness is founded in our understanding of who we are spiritually, relative to our human conditioning. This involves being present and mindful, which allows your spiritual nature to be remembered. The key is remembering the reality of the present moment. Being mindful of the now is elevating and puts you in touch with the spiritual faculties needed to live life consciously. These spiritual faculties include the releasing power of forgiveness, the practice of nonattachment, and using the conscious mind to approach fear with awareness so it can be neutralized as it arises.

The cultivation of self-awareness is a continuous process that requires experiencing negative thoughts and emotions, as they serve as signals to remember to reawaken. Understanding that this reality is one of contrast and polarities invites acceptance into the "isness" of the human experience, allowing you to move beyond the frustration that often comes with negative emotions.

From an awakened point of view (the awareness of stillness), negative emotion is not even recognized as such—it's given no label when it arises. Movement on the surface of the mind is observed, not identified with nor labeled as good or bad—it just is. The reason it's not labeled is that one knows their spiritual nature and the true nature of reality—it's all spiritual, it's all an extension of you, and it's a temporary reflection. With this clarity, one sees the futility in judging anything, as it leads to self-judgment because the truth of the matter is that we're all one.

Ten Daily Inner Balance Reminders

I'm now going to share ten daily reminders that can assist you and remind you to come back into balance as you navigate daily life. You can view them as signals designed to point you back to awareness, back to yourself. Refer to them as often as you need to.

- Balance negativity with positivity. The key is knowing when negativity arises and then taking the inner action to challenge it with a positive, life-affirming thought. Giving no belief to the negativity neutralizes fear and invites inner balance. As you affirm the positive thought, do so with conviction.

- Cultivate gratitude. The practice of giving thanks throughout the day is incredibly elevating. As it raises your vibrational frequency, it invites other high-vibrating and life-giving thoughts and ideas to arise.

- Inner peace is at your core. Remember that inner peace is what your inner being reflects, always. Be mindful that even if fear or anxiety arises, through your awareness of the now, it will not be able to last long. The experience of negativity does not change your spiritual nature.

- Observe the thinking mind. It's our identification with the ego, which comes disguised as the past and the future, that perpetuates suffering. By observing thoughts and emotions, rather than reacting to them, you starve fear and rise in consciousness.

- Prioritize self-care. It's vital to make time for yourself, especially in today's modern world. Setting time aside to self-reflect or to engage in self-healing practices such as meditation or listening to peaceful, high-vibration music, is balancing and renewing.

- Eat consciously. Being mindful about one's eating habits and knowing when to cut back or focus on more nutritional food choices starves gluttony and re-energizes the body. Having a balanced approach and including more fresh, organic/non-gmo foods is a positive step forward.

- Practice breathing. Taking just a few minutes a day to practice deep, slow breathing can prove to be rejuvenating and assist you in times where more stress is encountered.

- Practice forgiveness. Nothing is more powerful in releasing us from the past and from anger than the extension of forgiveness. In forgiving others, and ourselves in the process, we release the density of anger and other negative emotions associated with it.

- Stay active. The physical body is a vessel for the divine, and we honor ourselves when we take care of it. Spending 20 to 30 minutes a day walking, weightlifting, or doing your favorite exercise relieves stress and promotes well-being.

- Meditate daily. Spending ten minutes a day in silence and focused on the present moment can be incredibly transformative and renewing. As you cultivate your meditation practice, you can come to a point where you make every moment a meditation—this practice is one of personal mastery.

Emotional Triggers and Trauma

Negative emotions tied to previous traumas can keep us chained to the past when those very emotions haven't been addressed and faced. I am not for one moment tying to negate what one has gone through in the past. But rather, I want to reveal that we don't have to allow the past to dictate our present or our future by remaining there energetically. My goal is to show you that emotional triggers and trauma can be catalysts for awakening and healing when one is ready to forgive and release. Being ready is the key.

When a traumatic event or relationship is experienced, the energy associated with those experiences essentially attach to the person being affected. We're spiritual beings operating through and within universal energy, which includes positive and negative energies, so when our minds are unguarded because of our age (when we're young) or because of a lack of awareness, we're open to energy attachments. These energy attachments come in the form of emotions and are projected as anger, fear, resentment, guilt, and even feelings of distrust. Because of our human conditioning, these emotions are misunderstood and even taken as being who we are, once they've hijacked our consciousness. These very same emotions, either in the back of our mind or at the surface, dictate one's behavior and actions, whether one is aware of them or not.

When left to grow—through consistent reactions and triggers, which are reminders of the trauma—these energy attachments allow emotional pain to become heavier over time. Those who haven't discovered mindfulness approaches to dealing with and transmuting emotional pain turn to other ways to dealing with their suffering. Some go down the path of using substances or alcohol to numb oneself, which only perpetuates the cycle of suffering.

For some, pain can lead to awakening—to snapping out of negative habits. With understanding and taking a step back, even momentarily to see the bigger picture of why we experience such traumas, opens the door, even if it's just a crack, toward clarity. I can attest to the fact that being given a cancer diagnosis was traumatic. I was shocked and dismayed for several weeks after being diagnosed. I didn't understand what caused it or why it was happening to me, at the time.

As we accumulate layers of negative energy through traumatic events, and the triggers that follow, know that there is potential in the suffering we experience. The heaviness, sadness, depression, and anxiety that come from trauma can lead you to a moment where you decide you've had your fill and it's time for change. In other words, when you're ready—to look at the emotions, prepared to forgive those who've trespassed against you, and return to the power and strength of your inner being, choosing to no longer be a victim to the past—it's in that instant that massive change can take place. Every adversity, every failure, every trauma is not a reflection of your weakness but a testimony of your strength because life gives these challenges to those who are meant to transform and evolve—those who are meant to transform themselves, thereby changing the world for the better.

I want to remind you that the trauma took place in a past/present moment. By identifying with the past and its negative emotions and allowing them to be projected into the future through reaction, the suffering is being replayed in your mind. In order to free yourself, you must bring awareness to the thoughts and emotions that are continuing the suffering and decide to see them for what they are: the ego in disguise, the unconscious aspect of oneself.

The truth of the matter is that the ego takes every experience, good or bad, integrates it into its belief system and then spins it, making one see the past in only one way. Understandably, it's difficult to see the good in a traumatic event, and even more impossible to see the perfection in it, when one is in the middle of suffering. But know that these adversities come with a purpose, and it's not that we suffer perpetually, but rather that we awaken to the source of the suffering so healing can take place and you can become a candle bringing light to someone else's darkness through demonstration, to be of service.

The thing about the spiritual path, and personal growth in general, is that it's often quite turbulent and messy—and it's designed that way. Personal change never takes place when we're comfortable. With regard to trauma and the triggers that perpetuate it, know that the triggers can be seen from another point of view, one through clarity, that shifts them from being a source of pain to a reminder to awaken and even reawaken.

◎ Trigger and Trauma Healing Exercise ◎

The following healing exercise is geared toward going within and looking at the images, emotions, and triggers that perpetuate suffering so you can examine them, creating the potential for healing and even a spontaneous awakening. If you're ready to heal from trauma, this might be for you. If you're not ready, disregard this exercise until you are ready.

This exercise takes about ten to fifteen minutes, and it can be done once to twice weekly, depending on your readiness to shift beyond the past.

To begin, find a quiet space and get in a comfortable position. Preferably, sitting up straight with your head erect.

Close your eyes and take five to six deep breaths, relaxing into the moment. Drop your shoulders. Remind yourself as you're doing this that the present moment is all there ever really is—this instant, the now.

Now, take a few more breaths. As you relax and let go further, remember that you are a powerful spiritual being that understands that adversity, including traumas, are experienced in life but do, in fact, serve a greater purpose.

When you are centered and present, look within. Scan for the emotions and triggers that have been perpetuating the trauma. If and when you encounter them, don't react, instead observe them. Just be a space of awareness to witness them. Do this for two to three minutes.

Once you've observed the emotions and images/potential triggers, identify them. What are they being masked as? Is it anger? Is it fear? Is it hate? Is it worry? For the next minute or so, just label them.

When you've labeled them, take note of what you're feeling in your body. Just observe any sensations that arise. You don't have to fear them nor react to them. Just be the presence that is aware of the feelings. Do this for three to four minutes.

Once you've identified, observed, and felt the triggers and emotions, you can now choose to release them, thereby taking away their power.

Take a negative image or trigger and convert it to a word in your mind. If the trigger has been anger, see the word *anger* in your mind. If it's been fear, see the word *fear* in your mind.

With the word before you, speak the following to it with gentle conviction, two to three times: (You can prerecord the following, and then recite it during this part of the meditation.) "I am no longer going to be ruled by you. I am reclaiming my power now. I release and forgive you. I forgive myself. I forgive and release (*insert person's name if needed*). You no longer serve me, and I will not fear you because I understand what you are and who I am. I am the light, and you are the unconscious aspect of me that's been perpetuating suffering. I surrender you to the light."

When you're done, take a few deep breaths, open your eyes, and let the images and moment go. Know and understand that by doing this exercise, you're facing, dissolving, and thereby taking away the trauma and the trigger's power over you. You are reclaiming your vital energy and getting your power back. If and when the trigger or trauma reappears because of the energy it has accumulated, know that it's only an echo, a shell of the past. Continue to observe, as you starve the negative emotion and step back into your strength. Give thanks for release and healing.

Self-Love Is Healing

The journey of self-healing is the return to love—the unconditional love of spirit. This process is an unfolding one, as you let go and peel away the emotions, roadblocks, and trauma that have kept you feeling separate from Source Energy (oneness) and the healing that is directly experienced in stillness.

Self-love is based in self-understanding. It's knowing you're not the darkness but the light that temporarily took it on, so you could experience being human and the separateness that comes from the experience. Awakening reveals to you the reality of your inner being, which is unconditional love. By merging your awareness with the soul, you identify with spirit and all of its beautiful attributes. It's within this expanded, clear, and light-filled awareness that ego-identification dissolves and you're immersed in pure consciousness.

In this state of gratitude and appreciation for knowing the authentic self, self-love dissolves thoughts of self-hate, self-loathing, and self-judgment, replacing these negative emotions with self-forgiveness. It's by forgiving oneself, releasing the past and who you thought you were, that you free yourself, allowing your spiritual self to rise up through the chakras and to your conscious mind. Forgiveness is powerfully healing and drives out energies unlike itself. By breaking down the walls of the ego, forgiveness returns your awareness back to wholeness and the healing found in its foundation: the unconditional love of your inner being.

Eight Ways to Practice Self-Love

There are many ways to practice self-love, and here are eight ways to cultivate it—to point you toward your authentic self, where love abounds. Following these tips, I'm going to offer a meditation geared toward unconditional love awareness and recognizing its expression. Reflecting on these ways to practice self-love will further expand your awareness of it, shifting you toward the oneness of your inner being.

- Be gentle with yourself. The way you think and talk to yourself determines the way you feel. The more you understand yourself and what the ego is relative to you, the more compassion and kindness you'll extend inwardly, through clarity. The wonderful thing about this is that by being gentle with yourself, you'll to extend the same to others, elevating your relationships.

- Practice self-forgiveness. The healing journey is a process, and there can be times when one stumbles—that's part of being human. Thankfully, we've been given the gift of forgiveness, which releases us from our own transgressions, wiping our slate clean and allowing us to be renewed in mind and heart.

- Cultivate self-appreciation. Looking at how far you've come— the challenges and adversities that you've endured and faced— should remind you to give yourself a pat on the back and appreciate your strength and perseverance.

- Be self-centered. Here is a reminder that you can't be much help to others if you're stretching yourself thin, being a people-pleaser, or not being true to yourself. Being mindful of priorities, having healthy boundaries, and doing what you find meaningful by being your authentic self is love-based self-centeredness.

- Don't wait for happiness. Choosing to be happy, intentionally, without an external reason, is how you consciously cultivate the ability to raise your vibrational frequency on command. But don't stop there. You can also choose joy, bliss, and a grateful attitude simply by becoming that which you decide upon and become, energetically.

- Check in often with yourself. Being mindful of how you're feeling, and when you're not feeling your best, affords you the ability to shift out of an undesired state much quicker and with greater efficiency, through awareness. This practice can become automatic, over time, as you further cultivate mind-body awareness.

- Invite meditation into your moments. Meditation is simply focus, and being focused on the present moment with whatever task is before you allows your inner being—beingness—to merge with doingness, thereby elevating your experience.

- Use forgetfulness as a reminder. Understanding the undesirable impacts of negative thoughts and emotions can take those sources for feeling stuck or fearful, and use them as reminders to reawaken, forgive, release, and move forward. This is how one practices the art of inner balance—transmuting the dark with the light of awareness.

⑥ Self-Love Chanting Meditation ⑥

This is a very easy, fun, and light meditation. Find a quiet space and get comfortable, sitting or lying down is fine. Close your eyes, take three or four deep breaths, and relax into the present moment.

As you relax, shift yourself into a state of gratitude for who and what you are, and for what you've overcome in your life up until now. Just take two to three minutes to reflect on your spiritual journey and offer yourself the much-deserved gratitude you're owed.

Once you're done reflecting with kindness and gentleness, speak the following to yourself, three times: (You can prerecord this to play back as a guide, if you don't remember the chant.) "I am love, I am light, and I extend that love and light to myself. I forgive myself and release myself, now and when needed. I am kind and gentle with myself, now and always. Being love, I extend what I am to others."

When you're done chanting, offer gratitude once more to yourself. "I give thanks for who and what I am." Take a few deep breaths, open your eyes, and come back to your surroundings.

This meditation should only take five to eight minutes, and it can be done a few times a week or even once daily. It's a great way to practice self-love while raising your vibrational frequency. If you feel inspired, you can add to the chant as you see fit.

Healing As You Go

The key to maintaining inner balance is to face and neutralize negativity as it arises within your consciousness. It's only when left unchecked that negative thoughts and emotions build momentum, creating an energetic imbalance within that then reflects without. The way to nip negativity in the bud is to gauge how you feel throughout the day. By bringing awareness to the mind-body, you can assess whether or not you're feeling negativity, stress, or tension, thereby addressing the contraction of energy, right there, in the moment.

The great thing about practicing and cultivating awareness is that the closer you shift toward aligning with your inner being, the more obvious negative, egoic patterns become. This unfolding of clarity is your inner guidance system becoming more activated as your spiritual nature's baseline is stillness—the state of no-mind, no-thought.

As you become one with spirit—consciously—you integrate your physical senses more and more with your sixth sense (your intuition), which is always speaking to you through feeling. The way this works is as you observe negativity and challenge negative thinking, you subtract layers of human conditioning, allowing the intelligence of consciousness to come forward.

The more you practice and develop awareness, by letting fear and negative thoughts go, the more positive momentum you'll create, allowing the full expression of your spiritual self to develop. When the spiritual self is realized, it will merge with your local or conscious mind and fill the physical body with light. In this enlightened state, one is now operating through their highest self, in communion with it, moment by moment. It's this high-vibrational state that consumes negativity and fear as it presents itself. Because unconditional love is one's vibrational frequency, nothing in alignment with it can last long. The state of complete wholeness that you're operating through—oneness as mind, body, and soul—becomes one through the dissolution of the egoic, thinking mind.

Awakening Throughout the Day

Before awakening, the ego serves us as our personal identity, making up a large part of our personality. Taking on an ego causes our forgetfulness of spirit and allows for the experience of being human. Over time, as it's allowed to grow through reaction, it becomes darker and eventually becomes the source of our suffering—as emotional pain, dis-ease, and the feeling of being stuck. What starts out as being one's identity evolves to become one's source of suffering, which makes it, ultimately, the catalyst for awakening—the experience of ego death.

But the ego doesn't stop serving us post-awakening. Through the clarity of inner stillness, the ego, which was once the source of suffering, is now stripped of your vital energy and becomes a reminder to awaken, to come back to the present moment.

The practice of negating the ego and the dis-eased thinking it projects allows the ego to die, in the moment, allowing for consciousness to rise and reawaken you. Understanding the negative effects on the mind-body due to ego identification is the reason it's vital to reawaken throughout the day. In other words, your conscious mind—your awareness—is the guard that is shutting the ego out from impressing its negativity, fears, and nightmares upon your consciousness. If the guard falls asleep, even temporarily, the ego hijacks the individual, and one is back to experiencing third-dimensional consciousness. However, if one has cultivated a certain degree of awareness, spiritual faculties will spring forth, reminding one to shift out of the dreaming state and back to the reality of the here and now.

Applying mindfulness as you go about your day by letting things go and allowing negative emotions to die that no longer serve you through nonresistance, is the practice of mastery. It is a subtracting process, as you release negativity and its density, you come more into your authentic, spiritual self and let more go. Nothing has to be added, but rather the limiting thoughts, emotions, and ideas about ourselves and where we really are, need to be examined consciously so that one can decide whether to release them or continue to embrace them.

Morning Mantras

Using a mantra can really help you set a positive tone for the day and assist you in building momentum as you focus upon and manifest your desires. You can also revisit your morning mantra throughout the day to remind you, shift you, and refocus you. Be mindful that there's power in directing your mind in a life-affirming way, especially when you're speaking something into existence.

A great mantra should be inspiring and create forward-moving, high-vibrating feelings within you. It should include how you want to feel and what you desire to experience. As you state your mantra, say it with conviction and knowing, which is more powerful than belief, while being non-attached to outcomes—that is key.

I'm now going to offer you four sample mantras you can use every morning. The first is focused on improving health and increasing vitality. The second is a general mantra for various facets of your life. The third mantra focuses on relationships. And the fourth is geared toward alignment with abundance. Feel free to tailor these mantras or come up with your own. The important thing is to resonate with and feel what's being said with a sense that it's a present reality—that it's done.

Health Mantra

"I am healthier and stronger every day. I look and feel younger and more vital now and always. Every cell is happy, healthy, and functioning optimally within me. I am whole and complete. I am the embodiment of perfect health. Every day I'm moving toward greater health, happiness, and peace in mind, body, and soul."

General Mantra

"I am already having a wonderful day filled with health, happiness, abundance, and miracles. Things are always working out for me. I approach today with gratitude and appreciation as I move toward my dreams. I am divinely guided, empowered, and equipped to navigate life confidently, now and always. I am more than capable."

Relationships Mantra

"I am at peace with myself, everything, and everyone. I am kind, compassionate, and understanding. I am experiencing harmony, happiness, and joy in my relationships. I am present and aware in my daily interactions, and I am a great listener. I am forgiving, and I am grateful for forgiveness. I am authentic now and in the context of all my relationships."

Abundance Mantra

"I am abundant and prosperous, now and always. I am abundant in peace, happiness, clarity, wisdom, and joy. I am already wealthy, and I am experiencing increases in financial abundance, now and always. I am able to be of greater service through my abundance. I am grateful and wealthy in every facet of my life."

Approaching Stress Consciously

Stress is a state of reaction that is fueled by the ego, projected as worry and fear, and experienced as a contraction of energy and inner conflict. When we're experiencing stress, it's usually because we've shifted out of our centeredness by giving our attention and energy to another person, event, or circumstance. In essence, it's negative energy that's been compounded.

Stress can be triggered by numerous things—difficulties at work, relationship issues, illness, or financial troubles. Without understanding what the outside world is relative to us and that challenges are actually opportunities to grow, the conditioned response is to focus, thereby amplifying the unwanted situation in our minds. This invites all kinds of negative emotions, all of which lead to the experience of being stressed.

With clarity and understanding, stress can be approached consciously by getting to the root of the issue—the ego and its outlook on a perceived problem. Keep in mind that the ego can only project what it is—fear, worry, anxiety, confusion, and uncertainty—and these are major contributors to stress. Convincing its host that the problem is "out there" can leave one feeling helpless. But the issue is not external, it's the thinking that has painted it so. With every challenge we're presented, know that there's something bigger at play—a purpose to the adversity. Usually, it is hard to see when we're in the middle of the storm, but once it passes, hindsight or retrocognition offers clarity.

For the most part, challenges, and the stress that comes with them, can be diffused with the understanding that we're being directed or redirected to something greater. So many times, I've heard of people hitting roadblock after roadblock or experiencing a traumatic event, only to be transformed by them, which ultimately led them to fulfilling their destiny, their soul purpose. Personally, I've gone through several fires, some where there appeared to be no way out. But with perseverance and determination, these personal fires revealed their purpose in coming into my life.

The purpose of stress, from a spiritual point of view, is to crack the shell of the ego by showing you the futility in reacting and in operating primarily through third-dimensional consciousness. A moment of stress can be a pivotal point in one's life, where you decide you've had your fill of fear, frustration, and reaction and are ready to let them all go. Bringing awareness to stress, as the thoughts sponsoring the reaction arise, is how to diffuse and manage the stress, consciously.

Recognizing when fear is trying to build momentum, choosing to observe the emotions, and being present as they are energized is how to remain centered during moments of stress. The key elements to remember and cultivate in these moments of adversity are faith, trust, and the spirit of surrender. By doing so, you shift your belief away from fear and choose to offer it to these three powerful, spiritual forces.

⑥ Stress-Releasing Exercise ◎

We're now going to look at a stress-releasing exercise that was created to further cultivate your awareness while offering a strategy to manage stress consciously. This exercise should only take ten to fifteen minutes or so, and it can be referred to as needed or practiced proactively on a weekly basis. Its purpose is to remind you that your inner world is what paints the outer, and that with understanding you can approach challenges with greater confidence.

You'll need to be in a quiet area so you can focus. A pen and pad of paper or an electronic device will be needed to jot down insights.

We're going to start by looking at the arising issue or circumstance from an expanded point of view because emotions will never really give us the truth about a situation.

Take a few deep breaths, close your eyes, and drop your shoulders. As you come into a more relaxed state, you're going to remind yourself of the following: (You can record these spiritual reminders ahead of time and play them back when you're ready to.) "The outer world is a reflection of my inner world. Circumstances have no meaning, except the meaning I'm giving them. What may appear as a bad situation or an undesirable circumstance may very well be preparing me to expand my consciousness and grow further. It's the ego's need to control circumstances, people, or situations that causes reaction. I can choose to trust the process and, by doing so, surrender by being nonresistant as I cultivate faith and trust as I move forward. In the unseen, a way has already been made, I just have to choose it and align with it, energetically. I can choose to take conscious action, now, mentally and outwardly, in a positive way, for I am no victim to circumstance. I am letting go of the how and when, as I choose to flow."

Listen or reflect on the reminders that have just been offered for a few minutes.

Once you're done listening/reflecting, place your awareness on the arising situation or circumstance. Look at it from a spiritual perspective for a minute or two, remembering that you're always guided, and that there's a purpose in everything.

At this point, you can open your eyes and ask yourself the following: "Why is this circumstance being painted negatively? What can I do internally, and in the outer, to diffuse, lighten, and transcend the situation? How is stressing over this situation helping me?" Reflect on these questions for a few minutes, and then allow yourself to be inspired and guided toward a solution.

When you've received answers, make note of them and see if they resonate with you. Divine guidance will always show up as a high-vibrating feeling, and it will feel expansive, even supportive. If you haven't received any answers, don't fret. Put the paper / pen / device aside and come back to it later in the day or even the next day. I've come to understand that answers seem to arrive when one is ready to receive them.

If clarity has arrived in the form of a solution, give thanks. If nothing has come through, you can still choose to give thanks for the incoming solution and come back to the questions later. Take a few deep breaths, as you remember that circumstances are what we make of them and are malleable to our intentions, desire, and will, because they're experienced within our minds.

Simplify Your Life

Only you are the best judge for what you can tackle in any given day. You're the one responsible for yourself and for your well-being, and that makes you the best gauge for what needs to be addressed today and what can wait.

What I'm trying to make clear is that you have the power to make your life as simple or as busy as you wish. It's all about priorities. For some, living a simple life with minimal wants and desires is ideal. For others, there's a desire to enjoy the finer things in life. Both are valid decisions that can be experienced in a balanced way with prioritization and cultivation of self-awareness—nonattachment being key.

Part of simplifying your life is to let go of a people-pleasing mentality and create healthy boundaries. Choose what resonates with you, what excites you—the things that you're passionate about. Recognize who nurtures and supports you, and who doesn't. You're free to let go of those who don't; it's all about alignment and resonance.

You can still be empathetic and compassionate toward others while keeping them at a distance. The decision to simplify your life starts with deciding to look after yourself first—to be self-centered—not in an egotistical sense, but from the understanding you can only be of assistance to others when you're operating on all cylinders, centered in your vital energy.

Self-Care Is Healthcare

Being mindful and aware of how you feel, choosing high-vibrating thoughts and feelings proactively, and tending to the wholeness of your being is self-care. This self-empowering approach to living is how one takes care of their mental, emotional, physical, and spiritual health. Choosing how you wish to feel in the moment consciously, without waiting for something external to be the source of it, is not only a powerful expression of who you are spiritually but also reality changing in a very good way. Being aware of how you operate and taking self-correcting action, be it mentally or through outer steps, are the keys to well-being.

Choosing happiness now, without attachment, interestingly, is what will attract more external experiences to be happy about. The same goes for gratitude. Being grateful now, for who you are in Source and for health, clarity, wisdom, and divine guidance, shifts you into a reality where you experience more and more of these spiritual gifts.

Cultivating positive thinking and higher-vibrating feelings, such as joy and bliss, through present-moment awareness is a powerful way to shift your vibrational frequency, which positively impacts your overall well-being. As you do this, you invite more and greater feelings, further elevating your field of vibration. All of this practice positively affects the mind-body, strengthening your immune system and resiliency.

Ten Self-Care/High-Vibrating Affirmations

The following ten affirmations are designed toward self-care and feeling good now. Be mindful when you think and speak these affirmations that you can become them now, energetically. You don't have to wait for anything outside of you to change. These affirmations can be expressed daily and throughout the day as you desire. Here they are:

- I am happy now. I am happiness because I choose it.
- I love myself unconditionally, and I extend love and compassion to myself always.
- I am peace because that is what my soul is—now and forever.
- I am healthy in mind, body, and soul.
- I appreciate and honor this physical body as a vessel to explore the manifested world.

- I am kind and understanding to myself.
- I am grateful for this physical body and its ability to heal and renew.
- I am joy and bliss. I am the being that extends these attributes.
- I am mind, body, and spirit, and I am grateful for existing.
- Everything always works out for me, as I embrace the forces of faith, trust, and the spirit of surrender.

Chapter Ten
Conscious Eating through Awareness

As important as our food choices are, whether they are better for you (higher vibrating) or not so light (lower vibrating), so are the sponsoring thoughts, emotions, and awareness behind them. This should be mentioned right from the start: *good* or *bad* are relative terms, so it's vital not to label food as such because our perception of anything, including food, alters them since everything is a reflection of our consciousness. There's nothing wrong with having comfort food once in a while or fulfilling a craving—it's all about balance—and the awareness of knowing when we're making conscious and unconscious nutritional decisions.

My educational background is in science—dental hygiene and education—I'm no nutritional authority, but what I am adept in is the mind-body connection, listening to what the body requires and approaching nutrition from a conscious, awareness-based point of view. From this knowledge, I'll shed light on the ego and one of its facets (gluttony), highlighting subtle body alignment and how to tune in to its guidance regarding the topic of eating.

By looking at both sides of the coin, the way the ego and the subtle body approach food, one can only further expand their awareness and become more mindful in the process. We'll put a spotlight on how to look at food from a more conscious approach to empower you to make more conscious food choices and to see food beyond the good/bad perspective.

I've had challenges balancing my diet in the past, and I understand the emotional connection to making not-so-healthy food choices when feeling unfulfilled. When there's an aspect of our lives that appears empty or unsatisfactory, the conditioned response is to fill that space of emptiness with something, and for some, it's food.

Food, especially food that we really crave—the sugary or high-calorie type—seems to provide a temporary reprieve from feeling "less than" in a certain aspect of one's life. These habitual choices can become a pattern leading to repetitive cycles, further unhappiness, and even greater feelings of dissatisfaction, all which lower a person's vibrational frequency and disconnect one further from the subtle body.

What's disempowering in the process of consistently choosing less-than-healthy food options is the emotions and motivation behind those choices. As one feeds their emotions, they are also feeding the ego, energizing it by aligning with the energies of gluttony. Because of its insatiable nature, being in unconscious alignment with gluttony—an energetic aspect of the ego—leaves one in a constant state of craving, which leads to day-long snacking in between meals.

The vibrational field of gluttony is one that is voracious, leaving one never feeling satisfied. Operating from this lower-vibrational frequency leads to not only an energetic imbalance but also to imbalances within the body, which eventually can lead to symptoms.

Awakening to the egoic energy of gluttony begins with self-awareness—awareness of how one has been operating and becoming conscious of the unquenchable energies that come from this vibrational field. Becoming aware when gluttony presents itself (it's an overtaking energy that hijacks one's consciousness to overindulge) is where one begins the process of healing from it.

Becoming aware of the emotions fueling it, through self-reflection, and discovering where one feels unfulfilled are ways to get to the root of the problem. Being honest with ourselves, activating forgiveness if necessary, and addressing the aspect(s) of our lives that we feel a void in, through conscious action, are the beginning steps to coming back into balance, energetically and physically.

A more conscious approach to food and food choices starts by breaking the mental connection within that says food is a friend or the sole source of comfort when stressed. Becoming aware of one's need for food as a comfort interrupts the cycle of suffering—overindulging. In other words, awareness is everything.

Looking at food differently—primarily as the way to fuel the body—shifts you away from seeing it as a way to be temporarily fulfilled. From this more neutral point of view, which is that of the subtle body, one can make more conscious choices as one becomes more mindful of the body's needs.

When one is more ego/gluttony focused, the food choices are primarily concentrated on the emotional needs, as one seeks to feel better and get relief through eating. However, this is a trap because poor food choices, and consistent ones at that, lead to more of the same, and eventually lead to feeling even worse. Conversely, when you're more in alignment with the soul, you're clearer in being able to discern and connect with what the subtle body and, ultimately, the physical body require nutritionally speaking. In other words, the ego seeks temporary fulfillment, while the soul/subtle body seeks fuel for the long term.

Becoming more subtle body aware is a matter of placing your attention inward and becoming more in tune with what you're feeling, in this case regarding food and nutrition. The subtle body is always in communication with your conscious mind, and being aware of this shifts you closer in alignment with its divine intelligence and guidance. The subtle body's approach to diet and food is a spiritual one. To further understand it, the subtle body is transcendent of cravings and is discipline itself, in a sense, when it comes to eating. It sees food as fuel that assists in maintaining health and inner balance.

If you want to know how to make more conscious food choices for what your body needs, contemplate two different food choices—one that fulfills a craving or an emotional need and one that you know is higher vibrating and more nutritionally sound— and pay attention to how the body responds with each potential choice.

If you've become more in tune with the body through mindfulness, the body reacts in a negative fashion, contracts in fact, when the denser or emotional food choice is reflected upon. When the more conscious, higher-vibrating food choice is focused upon, a lighter, more receptive feeling is experienced. Applying this approach can not only help guide you in making more conscious food choices but also assist in the development of one's mind-body connection.

Food Labels

I want to wrap up this section by addressing the labels placed on food, especially one that is disempowering. Of course, certain food choices have to be labeled for clarity's sake, such as lower-vibrating, denser, unconscious choices versus higher-vibrating, lighter, conscious choices. These relative labels are not the issue—the issue is labeling food as "junk."

I want to bring awareness to the power one has to negatively impact food through thinking or speaking negatively about it. Remember that what one projects or expresses, one becomes in that moment. Calling something "junk food" has a negative connotation to it, thereby impacting one's vibrational frequency whether they're aware of it or not. If you have to label a food choice or an unhealthy snack, you can refer to it as a "cheat meal" or "cheat snack," which energetically softens the blow, so to speak.

We're always calling forth our reality through our thoughts, words, and feelings, including our outlook. Being more conscious of our word choices is just another way to maintain or raise our vibrational frequency. It's about remembering just how powerful we are, and how we can focus and place our energy more toward what serves us.

Ten Ways to Practice Conscious Eating

We're now going to look at ten ways to become more mindful and make more conscious, nutritionally sound food choices. Take what resonates and leave the rest. You're always free to revisit, and make changes as you see fit.

- When you find yourself wanting to snack, ask the self-reflective question "Am I bored, feeling emotionally unsatisfied, or truly hungry?" More often than not, the answer will arrive before you even finish posing the question.

- Plan your meals. Doing some meal preparation or thinking ahead and choosing what you'll consume in the coming day can help you remain focused.

- Set a goal. Choosing to shed some pounds and become healthier through more-conscious food choices gives the mind the much-needed direction it desires. It also comes with the bonus of feeling better through lighter, higher-vibrating, less-processed food choices. Remember, balance is key.

- Drink more water. Staying hydrated is important, and water is a natural appetite suppressant.

- Proactively begin the healing process of addressing your emotions and where you may feel unfulfilled in your life. Facing ourselves is not only courageous but also healing, as we bring to light the emotional roadblocks keeping us stuck and preventing us from living a fulfilling life.

- You're free to see food more as nutrition, and not so much as a comfort, if you wish. Using this approach aligns you more with the subtle body and softens the mind-food connection, allowing you to make more nutritionally sound choices.

- Make food choices through the present, not the past. New food choices require a renewed state of mind. Decide what you really need, not how you want to feel. Interestingly enough, when you begin to make more consistent and conscious food choices, you will naturally begin to feel a greater sense of well-being, as well as being more energized.

- When you do make "unhealthier" food choices, be mindful not to judge or label your choices negatively.

- Bless your food with gratitude just before you eat. Extending a blessing on anything, including food, is immediately returned to you.

- Chew your food and savor it. I don't count how many times I chew, but I ensure that while eating I am present, take my time, and enjoy the process with appreciation.

Eating with Gratitude

The practice of giving thanks before a meal and feeling gratitude while you eat elevates you and the overall experience. Being mindful as you eat and cultivating a spirit of thankfulness raises your vibrational frequency, making you feel greater harmony and an increased sense of well-being. When we're thankful for anything, we're opening the door to more experiences to be grateful for.

By combining mindfulness with gratitude while eating, you slow down and savor every bite of the meal, chewing your food more completely. This gives the body time to digest the food being consumed. With so many of us living fast-paced lives, eating mindfully with gratitude can remind us to shift into a more relaxed state and enjoy the present moment more fully.

Applying gratitude toward the food we eat, the people who grew it, the person or people who prepared it, and the person who served it, has a powerful, positive, far-reaching effect. As we extend gratefulness, it's immediately returned and experienced within us, elevating us. In the unseen, spiritual realm, there really are no small deeds, as every thought, emotion, and feeling is creative and ever-expanding. Coming from this awareness, one can see how transformative gratitude can be, even as it's expressed toward a meal.

As we shift into a more receptive and calm state through gratitude, we prepare our digestive system to function optimally. In 2019, Alicia Rennoll wrote an article for *Harvard Business Review* called "Gut Health Is Key to Your Mental Health at Work" that sums up this idea nicely. Rennoll wrote: "…you need to be able to digest food effectively—for which you must be in a parasympathetic state, also known as 'rest and digest.' When the body is not in this relaxed state, it cannot produce the gastric juices it needs to be able to adequately absorb food. This means that it won't be able to absorb vitamins, minerals, and nutrients required to be able to support a healthy body and brain."

This article also reminded me how important it is to practice being calm and in a relaxed, centered state as we navigate our day. When we're not in a stressed "fight-or-flight mode," we're clearer, more adaptable, and able to face challenges with greater confidence. Applying gratitude throughout our day, not just before or during a meal, reminds us how blessed we are, and to not take life too seriously. It lights us up and softens us as we shift toward a spirit of appreciation.

Balance Is Key

Like anything in life, it's important to maintain balance, as too much of any particular thing can throw one off energetically. When the mind is overwhelmed with negativity through past/future thinking, it calls for neutrality (through the present moment) and balance (through positive thinking). When the soul has been forgotten, we experience confusion and fear, and it calls to us, as it's desiring to be remembered through the experience of inner stillness, so we can come back to clarity and fearlessness. And when the physical body has taken in too much processed food, or has lacked nutrition and appreciation, those imbalances call for more nutrient-dense foods and an improvement in diet, self-love, and gratitude for the physical vessel provided for us.

Everything is always speaking to us. We must become aware of this fact and pay attention to the subtle and not-so-subtle cues. Imbalance of any kind is a messenger that says it's time to make a change, take action, and shift back into balance.

By paying attention to the subtle body's cues and the way we feel, more conscious choices can be made, as one comes into more alignment with the wisdom of the subtle body. Remember that the subtle body is all about maintaining balance, and when imbalance takes place nutritionally speaking, the subtle body will respond through feelings to advise what doesn't resonate with it. The wonderful thing about listening to these subtle cues, which come as instant knowings or energetic nudges, is that as you become more aware of them, you will cultivate your overall intuition more. As your intuition further develops, you will resonate and consciously align with the subtle body more.

Eight Tips to Cultivate Awareness

I have eight tips that will help you further cultivate your discernment regarding the wisdom and guidance that the subtle body offers to assist you in maintaining balance. The goal of these tips is to expand your awareness through the insights offered. Here they are:

- Check in with the way you're feeling often, especially when about to make food choices. Bringing your awareness inward and focusing on what you're feeling for thirty seconds at a time will develop subtle body connection.

- Proactively choose more unprocessed, nutritionally dense foods. This will almost always provide you with higher-vibrating feelings. By making note of those feelings, you can use them to recognize the contrast in the way you feel during and after eating processed foods.

- Allow yourself to become comfortable with feeling the highs, the lows, the higher vibrations, and the lower vibrations. Remember that no energy can harm you without your permission. We need to let go of the fear of emotions and realize that they are messengers that serve to inform us of when we're in/out of balance.

- The subtle body is always in communication with you. Becoming aware of this insight can open the door further to picking up on its cues. The key is to be present and in the moment.

- The quieter you become internally, the clearer the communication will be between the subtle body and your conscious mind. Cultivating a meditation practice by introducing meditation as you go about your day by just being focused in the here and now is a way to elevate your awareness toward stillness.

- The subtle body is designed to bring you back into balance automatically. It requires only one thing from us: to heed its guidance.

- The subtle body doesn't use fear to get its message across, but it will use heavier feelings and denser energies when foods are being chosen that are not in alignment with it.

- The subtle body communicates to you through the chakras. Being mindful of what each chakra represents energetically will assist you in becoming more subtle body aware, further developing your ability to read energy.

Insights on Food and Nutrition

You'll know how close in alignment you are with the subtle body as it pertains to food by the way you feel and how disciplined, or consistent, your approach is in making conscious choices. Like the soul, and this may sound dull, the subtle body is not moved by externals, and that includes our favorite comfort foods, including desserts.

From one point of view, it almost looks like a computer program that's designed to have the physical body operate optimally. When the program is mostly adhered to, we feel great and are full of energy. When the program is overwritten through consistent choices that are contrary to its innate intelligence, the program experiences issues. In the process, it will send subtle cues that are messengers asking us to come back to alignment. Being a contrasting energy to the ego, the subtle body is just that—subtle, lighter, and operating through a higher frequency, as it's an extension of the soul.

What I'm pointing to is: like attracts like. The ego is a denser, heavier energy because of its nature, and it seeks things, including foods, that resonate with it. The subtle body is a natural part of who you are (the soul), and it seeks sun-filled, lighter food that is higher vibrating and unprocessed—essentially unaltered. All of this reflects the world of duality, of contrast—and it's all a gift. These opposite energies provide us with differing perspectives and the freedom to choose. What we experience is based on our choices—all which serve us by providing us with experience.

What the subtle body wants to highlight here is that there really is no right or wrong choice. We have free will, and our conscious mind is at the center between the subtle body's divine intelligence and the cravings of the ego. Everyone's take on inner balance in terms of food and nutrition is going to look a little different, and that's more than okay. It's like we're each given a canvas, which is our life, and we are free to choose between the various colors, the darks and the lights. Your choices determine what you see in your painting, from the various facets of your life.

As one becomes more disciplined in their approach to food choices and overall nutrition, a lighter and greater sense of well-being will be felt. The reason for that is the choices begin to resonate more with spirit and the light-filled energies of the subtle body. The subtle body is the energetic representation of inner balance, wholeness, and health. Based in the unconditional love of the soul, the subtle body can and will bathe you in that love for brief moments, if it serves you, through the extension of gratitude for adhering to its guidance and wisdom. We are always responding or reacting to our decisions; the responding takes place with conscious choices and the reacting is through egoic-based decisions.

Five Ways to Align with the Subtle Body

I want to provide you with five more ways you can begin to tune in to the subtle body and its higher-frequency energies. These methods will make it easier for you to discern when you've shifted to be more in alignment with it. These insights are essentially reminders, pointing you inward toward your own inner knowing and intuition.

- Practice the art of listening and reading energy—yours and others. Bringing your attention and awareness to how you feel on a daily basis, cultivating empathy for others, and becoming a great listener are ways to hone your ability to be centered and focus. Through that centeredness, you're able to pick up on the subtle energy of the subtle body.

- Become mindful of the awareness that is experiencing the thinking mind. You experience thoughts and emotions, but those are always changing, fleeting. Your authentic self is the awareness experiencing them. Becoming aware of your very own awareness is the doorway back to the soul and the subtle body within it. This can be practiced by sitting quietly for a few minutes at a time and looking within.

- Know that you're already connected—you just have to cultivate that connection. Reflecting on what each chakra represents and embodying stability, playfulness, your inner power, unconditional love, speaking your truths, listening to your inner wisdom, and remembering the reality of oneness, aligns you more with your spiritual aspects.

- Let go of energy blocks by becoming aware of them. When we feel disconnected from our spiritual nature, it's often because we're holding on to things from the past—emotions that are calling to be released. Practicing exercises and meditations designed to assist you in releasing that which no longer serves you shifts you beyond the egoic layers of separation and toward your authentic, spiritual self.

- When choosing foods that are more in alignment with the subtle body, you're embodying more of your spiritual nature. As a result, you're resonating more with the subtle body. As you become more consistent in healthier food choices, you'll open yourself to more awareness and insights. It's like a flowering of consciousness taking place— an unfolding of awareness.

Nurturing the Physical

I want to close this chapter by talking about self-care from a self-nurturing point of view. Taking time for yourself, being physically active, getting fresh air and sunlight, knowing when to rest, and getting enough sleep are all ways to nurture not only the mind but also the physical body. The mind-body is a two-way communication system, which allows the physical body to communicate what it needs through sensations, feelings, even aches and pains. The key is being in touch with mind, body, and soul through mindfulness, which gives you the ability to read the information that the subtle body relays back to your awareness on behalf of the physical body.

An essential part of self-care is taking care of the physical body. This will also benefit you mentally, as these two aspects are deeply connected. Providing the body what it needs will pay you back dividends in the form of increased energy, greater mental clarity, better sleep, and overall greater strength. The physical body was created to allow you to experience feeling—positive and negative, highs and lows, exhaustion and rejuvenation, and everything in between. We honor the body when we use it in mindful, constructive, and positive ways to better improve ourselves, enjoy life, and express ourselves.

Addressing the body and its needs isn't a complicated process when we're already cultivating awareness and working toward inner balance. Paying attention to how we feel and taking the inner and/or outer action needed to address what's being called for—whether it's more water to hydrate ourselves, spending more time outside, or recognizing when and how to fuel the body—further cultivates mind-body awareness and discernment.

Eight Tips for Nurturing the Body

The following eight tips are meant to be reminders, highlighting some ways to nurture the physical body and ourselves in the process, further cultivating self-love and the mind-body connection.

- Practice being calm. Taking time to meditate, putting electronics away for periods at a time, doing calming activities such as reading or journaling, and practicing deep breathing a few minutes every day are all great ways to detach from the busyness of everyday life.

- Declutter and organize. Tidying up your surroundings is not only a good way to be active but can also bring you a tremendous amount of relief, as well as a feeling of accomplishment. Having an organized home allows you to be more comfortable in your surroundings, allowing you to relax mentally and more fully.

- Get creative. Expressing your creativity through a passion is a wonderful way to bring together mind, body, and soul. There are countless ways to express yourself, and some examples include drawing, painting, gardening, brainstorming a new invention, taking a trip, or creating a gratitude list.

- Stay hydrated. Drinking enough water daily is vital for many reasons. When we're hydrated, we have more energy, staving off fatigue. It also assists in flushing out toxins, improves digestion, and improves skin health. There are several more benefits to getting enough water, and knowing this should be your motivation to make sure you stay hydrated.

- Begin every day with gratitude. Starting the day off on the right foot sets the stage for how you'll navigate and experience the rest of your day. An attitude of gratitude not only nourishes the mind and soul but also every cell of the body. A light-filled energy, gratitude makes us feel happier and joyful.

- Balance your diet. Nourishing the body with organic, non-genetically modified, nutrient-dense foods fuels the body with much-needed vitamins, minerals, and amino acids. Making mostly mindful, body-aware food choices allows for the occasional indulgence without experiencing much, or any impact, I have found.

- Get sunshine daily. The sun's rays help your body produce vitamin D, which has numerous health benefits, including helping to maintain strong bones and muscles. Over the last several years, much fear has been created around sun exposure. Keep in mind what we have been examining throughout this book: what we believe, and what one fears, is what can be attracted. Having an awareness that the sun is your friend is an extension of consciousness and is nourishing shifts personal experience to a more positive one. Of course, also practice safe time exposures (when and how long).

I have found the most positive benefits come from spending time in the sun before noon and after four p.m.

- Give and receive hugs. Hugs not only feel good but are also great ways to reduce stress and affirm, or deepen, our connection with others. Hugs are also good for the heart, as they expand the heart chakra, allowing that energy to be expressed. Being hugged also has a calming effect on our minds and our nervous systems, as the act is an expression of love, which is healing in and of itself.

Chapter Eleven
A Paradigm Shift in Health

Fifth-dimensional health is a vibrational state of being centered around the awareness of who you are spiritually, encompassing all aspects of being—mind, body, and soul. This directly experienced, light-filled level of consciousness is the result of one's personal evolution—from the thinking mind to the dimension of inner stillness. A reflection of spiritual embodiment, this degree of health is tangible, in that it's experienced as ease, inner peace, a calm mind, clarity, and the vitality that comes from living as a spiritual being. A contrasting experience to third-dimensional consciousness, this level of health is based in self-responsibility that begins with the recognition of mind, body, and soul—and their interconnectedness.

As an active participant in your own health, through self-understanding and expanded awareness, you proactively take action on the level of mind because, as a self-actualized being, you understand that the body reflects your consciousness. Inner balance is practiced by observing negative thoughts and affirming positive ones, thereby raising your vibrational frequency, as the light of the soul is allowed to rise, shining greater awareness not only to just your mind but also your entire body.

What has just been described is the health that's experienced through the state of enlightenment. It's the divine state of health, where one has laid aside their limiting ideas about themselves, life, and what health means, allowing the higher mind and soul to remind you what it means to live as spirit—what spiritual embodiment reflects.

As I write this, the subtle body reminds me that it doesn't stop at physical health; being centered in the light of one's true consciousness—stillness—you are divinely guided in all aspects of your life and given insights and solutions as challenges arise.

Divine health is a result of the unrestricted flow of universal energy and its light to the chakra system, energizing and activating them fully. This process of renewal and rejuvenation fills the physical body with light, as now the subtle body has been remembered and allowed to shine through each and every cell.

In tuning in to the subtle body's energy, I am informed that more and more people are awakening to this evolved state of health. Millions of people are already awakening to the idea that there's more to themselves and more than meets the eye to the manifested world. As more human beings experience the ever-growing intolerability that is third-dimensional consciousness, with all of its fear, dis-ease, heaviness, and uncertainty, they have been and will continue to seek relief from it. The relief comes in the form of the present moment—the awareness of it—relative to the concepts of past and future.

Being in the present moment is a personal decision that requires one to become aware of the limiting energies and uneasiness offered by the past and the future, to shift awareness to the present, and to anchor one's awareness into the now.

People will seek out and eventually shift into fifth-dimensional consciousness to experience the health benefits of it because conventional medicine is proving to be outdated and unreliable. It has become outdated because we're all evolving and it hasn't kept up; energy medicine is the next evolutionary step because it's an aspect of the personal responsibility state known as enlightenment.

Conventional medicine has become unreliable because so many doctors are being overworked and underappreciated, with many choosing to relocate to where they're more valued. When this happens, it leaves deficiencies in particular areas, leaving them underserviced. It is also unreliable because, over the last few years, medicine has been hijacked by groups of powerful individuals who are not so interested in healing, but in profit. Don't get me wrong, there are amazing ethical doctors out there, but there is an influence that is third-dimensional based and, like a virus, has infiltrated the minds not just of healers but the entire planet—ego consciousness. What's being pointed to is not personal in any way, but is describing how virtually the entire planet is asleep to their true nature, and because of that has no understanding of what it means to embody supernatural health—the health of spirit.

I know in Canada, where I am, wait times for a specialist are quite long. I have heard of people dying while waiting to see one. According to a Fraser Institute article from 2022 by Mackenzie Moir titled "Waiting Your Turn, Wait Times for Health Care in Canada, 2022 Report," there's a "...median waiting time of 27.4 weeks between referral from a general practitioner and receipt of treatment." With my province, Ontario, having a "...total wait— 20.3 weeks—while Prince Edward Island reports the longest—64.7 weeks." Imagine having to wait more than a year to see a specialist.

I am reminded to share this message: Do not fret or worry with the changes taking place in the world, but remember that as human beings evolve, so will medicine—it will have no choice. The medicine of today will still be used for some time, and it will for even longer continue to be needed for emergencies until human beings shift completely and collectively into 5D consciousness, where one will be more spirit than material, where healing will be instant, only an intention away.

One more thing: Remember that change on any level can be somewhat turbulent at times, but with faith and trust, change can be approached with less fear and more certainty during this collective shift.

Set a Vision for Your Health and Life

In the last several years, I have seen so many people get caught up in and frustrated with the law of attraction. They are trying to manifest their dreams without fully understanding who they are spiritually and without awareness of the law of cancellation—how to dissolve and stop fear, doubt, and uncertainty from bringing their desires to fruition.

The law of cancellation is based in observation, nonattachment, and surrender; the ability to let go of how and when the desire will manifest. So much emphasis has been placed on attracting things—feelings, the right partner, abundance, material items—but virtually nothing has been said about how to address the fear that will inevitably attempt to stand in your way during the manifesting process.

It's vital that you understand your oneness with Source Energy and embody it by operating through awareness of this fact, in a moment-by-moment fashion, as you cultivate not only your desires but also the spirit of nonattachment and surrender in the process.

What's we're talking about here is the awareness and the ability to nullify fear and frustration during the manifesting process.

The law of cancellation refers back to the process of observing fear and negative emotion, challenging it with a positive thought, and then remembering the present moment. This process nullifies fear; when you starve fear of your energy and reaction, it has nothing to feed off. It may protest for a little longer; let it. Be not afraid of it whatsoever. Fear, which is the darkness we experience, is nothing without your belief; cancel it by stripping it of your life force and it will lose all its power. The truth of the matter is that it never really had any power to begin with; you only thought it did, and that's because of ego identification—thinking one is the fear.

Now that a foundation for greater awareness has been laid down for manifesting your life consciously through intention, the next step is to set a vision for your life based on knowing who you are and what's possible. This vision includes, but is not limited to, your state of mind, which includes inner peace, clarity, and understanding your health, your relationships, your finances, and your career. By understanding your oneness with Source and embodying spirit, you shift into fifth-dimensional consciousness through inner stillness—the unified field. Being one with the birthplace of miracles leads to the understanding that all things are possible. Your only job now is to decide and direct your life consciously as you cocreate with the higher mind and soul.

Once a vision has been set, it's important to remember not to be attached to the idea. Source, I have found, has a way of dreaming even bigger and operates spontaneously, which is why it's important to ensure you don't snag yourself in the energy of "waiting for something to happen." Becoming one with your desire includes imagining the wish as already fulfilled, feeling its manifested reality as you embody the desire, and immersing yourself in the image with gratitude and appreciation. As you energetically align with the desire, take the action you're divinely guided to take—to unite the unified field reality to the manifested world, being mindful to let go of how and when.

Cultivating the law of cancellation by observing and challenging negative thought at its inception while remembering the present moment, is one of the most, if not *the* most, powerful inner action you could take to raise your vibrational frequency and allow your dreams to come to fruition. Remember also that the key to embodying spirit is surrender; it's a level of trust so developed that you abandon your life to the spiritual forces within and without because you understand and know they are all for you. This kind of personal liberation is, in essence, otherworldly, with the faith being so cultivated and perfected that the result is having the faith of Source.

I didn't start consciously manifesting my life until I knew who I was, which led me to discover my passions, my purpose, and the cultivation of the spiritual tools and awareness to do so. What I have discovered is by tapping into our potentials, we bring to life desires and even dreams we never knew existed on some level within us. It is an unfolding process, as self-awareness is cultivated, gifts and talents are allowed to blossom.

Five Ways to Discover Your Passions and Purpose

I want to close this section with some tips on how to hone in on your passions and find your purpose. As you may find, it all ties in with vision setting and manifesting. Be mindful that the foundation to the process of bringing your desires to fruition is knowing who you are, being aware of the spiritual tools already in your possession, and bringing those tools to life, through inner and outer action.

- Find your soul purpose. Your purpose, first and foremost, is to remember who you are spiritually. In essence, that's why we all showed up here on earth: to temporarily forget, only to create the desire to remember. Once your soul purpose is realized and you're beginning to embody who you are spiritually, you may find that, as spiritual gifts, talents, and faculties come alive, you begin to remember what it is that you're supposed to share with others.

- Follow your passions. We don't have to limit ourselves in any way, and it's more than okay to know who you are spiritually while following your passions toward a particular career. From a spiritual point of view, it's not so much the doingness that is important, as what one is being. In other words, you can be an enlightened being who owns a bakery, is a police officer, or is a doctor. Here's a little secret: you are all already enlightened beings playing these roles—all of you. You've just forgotten temporarily; therefore, lighten up and follow your dreams.

- Create a vision board. Putting together a vision board can help you hone in on what you desire to experience and spark your imagination further, helping you becoming clearer and more focused. As you go through the process of sifting through potentials and possibilities, you may find you add or delete details, all which serve you toward greater clarity.

- Decide what's possible. The more you cultivate spiritual awareness and become aware of the dimension of inner stillness, the more you'll realize that all things are possible. This is a personal journey; allow yourself time to process the fact that when you're embodying spirit—vibrating through stillness—and thinking, speaking, and intending as such, that field of awareness allows miracles to express. Going one step further, through stillness, miracles are known to be the natural state of things—constantly taking place, not the exception.

• Cultivate your gifts. Some talents are natural and are known early on; others can be discovered later in life and may take time to be developed. Discovering what you really love to do, and working at it—honing it, expressing it, and sharing it with the world—is incredibly fulfilling. All of us have gifts to share; it's our job to go within, uncover them, and then bring them to life.

Spiritual Wellness

Embarking upon one's soul purpose is the most challenging, and yet most fulfilling, journey one could ever take. Beyond what anyone could achieve in the material world, remembering your spiritual self by awakening to the spiritual dimension within—stillness—takes the concept of success to an entirely different level.

Knowing who you are spiritually lays the foundation for spiritual wellness. As your purpose unfolds simultaneously with your awareness, you discover a deep sense of purpose, giving a profound meaning to not only your life but to all of existence.

Your values become clearer and your priorities may change or evolve to reflect your awareness of oneness, as the spiritual path is a process of remembering and self-discovery. The realization of the reality of oneness becomes a guiding principle, giving you direction toward being of service. The soul, having the desire to express itself, finds fulfillment in giving and sharing of itself. Knowing that abundance is the "isness" of life, the self-realized soul has transcended any and all thoughts of lack in remembering its source, which is unlimited.

Being mindful of what the soul desires to experience—first and foremost, it seeks self-actualization—the realization of its full potential is to express what it knows (through mind and body) in order to experience its creations. The soul, being a reflection of the All That Is, seeks to express all of its spiritual faculties and gifts, which include psychic abilities, through the outward flowing state of stillness.

Allowing inspiration to manifest spontaneously due to its nature, a mind that has realized the soul will work in concert with the physical body to share its potentials through various ways. For some, it's through music, art, or writing. Others may find fulfillment through teaching or volunteering their time. Regardless of the passion, the beingness is what precedes the doing—it's foundational in whatever task is taken up.

Eight Insights Toward Spiritual Wellness

Having laid a foundation for spiritual wellness and what it looks like, from the soul's perspective, I'm going to now offer eight tips to cultivate spiritual health and wellness. As you reflect on these insights, you may be inspired to cultivate and deepen your spiritual practice and wellness. Here they are:

- Live from within. Being present and centered, and through the understanding that you are the cause to your effects, reminds and empowers you to observe the inner world of thought. By that process, you allow the spiritual to reveal itself, within and without.

- Cultivate authenticity. Living true to yourself, remembering that you don't need to navigate the world through a defensive mindset, and letting go of the fear of what others think of you is not only liberating but also opens the door to effective and honest communication.

- Find your passions. Nothing is as energy-draining and joy-robbing as doing something you dislike or resent. We all have gifts to share, and for many of us, it takes first finding and resonating with our spiritual selves before those potentials can be shared with others.

- Allow creativity to flow. The soul is creative by nature, and it is teeming with brilliant ideas, inspirations, and potential. Your job is to get in tune with your creative side by going within and paying attention—as you're aware that divine guidance, including creativity, is always being offered to you.

- Be of service. Fulfillment comes by taking inspiration, using the mind to set out a plan, and then taking those elements and integrating them to the manifested world through action. If possible, find and do something every day that you find fulfilling, even if it's only for an hour or two. This may be working toward making a dream come true, volunteering, doing a favor for someone, or offering support to a friend or a family member.

- Choose happiness proactively. You don't have to wait for circumstances to change in order to experience happiness. Happiness, the kind that self-actualized people can call forth at will, is based in the knowing that what they choose is experienced in the moment. Choosing happiness by saying "I am happy" without an external attachment is how authentic happiness is cultivated.

- Make everything a meditation. This is the ultimate goal: to experience your inner being on a moment-by-moment basis, as it is the master meditator—silent by nature. You don't have to do anything except continue to choose to bring your awareness to your inner being—the stillness within. As you do so more and more, you'll invite stillness to blossom that much further into your moments and experiences.

- Your primary relationship should be with your self. Cultivating self-love, understanding, self-responsibility, and forgiveness creates the atmosphere for harmonious relationships with others. Being at peace with yourself first, you are at peace with the world, thereby changing it—you're that powerful.

Conclusion

Becoming aware of and working with the subtle body has the potential to guide you inward, toward the wholeness of your inner being—the soul itself. It's this elevated awareness that offers you the tools and means by which you can discern and tune in to divinely guided wisdom and information more easily, bringing you greater clarity on your healing journey.

We are spiritual and energetic beings first and foremost, and by remembering that, we can move forward toward inner balance on all levels—mind, body, and soul. As I write this, I want to remind you that the ego, and even the physical body, are not things to be afraid of but rather understood.

Seeing these elements that make us human as gauges to inner balance or the lack thereof, we can become empowered to take inner and outer action. This allows us the potential and possibility to return to wholeness and the healing found within it.

Many blessings on your healing journey,

Jiulio

Glossary

Attachment: An energy form that presents as a thought or an emotion; possessive in nature. See energy attachments.

Authentic self: One who is beyond the thinking mind; the soul or inner being.

Awakening: The process of becoming aware of the thinking mind and its true nature; the shift in consciousness from the dreaming state of thought (3D) to the dimension of inner stillness (5D).

Awareness: The increased ability to recognize and understand expanded levels of consciousness, spiritual faculties, and the higher mind.

Chakra: An energy wheel or center located within the subtle body that channels universal or cosmic energy; each chakra is associated with an organ or a particular region of the body.

Conditioned mind: The thinking mind that operates between past and future.

Conscious mind: A person's awareness of their immediate or local surroundings; also referred to as local mind; the positive aspect of one's mind.

Consciousness: The mind of Source; that which is all-encompassing, and where one operates from; also known as Source Energy.

Cosmic consciousness: The dimension of inner stillness, the mind of Source—transcendent of the thinking mind. See universal consciousness and fifth-dimensional reality.

Cosmic energy: The limitless and unending power that is all-encompassing, giving life to humans and all life forms; an extension of Source, also known as universal energy.

Dis-ease: A negative energetic state based in ego consciousness that, when left unchecked, can disrupt the body's intelligence, impacting one's mental and physical health; a vibrational frequency of uneasiness.

Dreaming state: The state of being solely identified with the thinking mind.

Ego death: The letting go of negative emotion; the end of the ego's control over one's consciousness; the shift from thinking to stillness, separation to oneness.

Embodiment: Spiritually speaking, the tangible expression of one's spiritual nature through direct experience and knowing.

Energetic nudge: An energetic prompting or instant download/knowing that comes from the soul, or subtle body, as divine guidance.

Energy attachments: These energies come in the form of negative emotions, feeding off of one's vital energy as they hijack a person's consciousness; these present often as chronic anger, hate, resentment, and guilt.

Energy field: The energy, which can be high or low vibrating, that one operates through and from.

Energy medicine: A field of alternative treatments that use intention while working with the individual's consciousness and the body's life force to clear energy blockages and restore inner balance.

Enlightenment: A state of being transcendent of thought; the direct, moment-by-moment experience with Source Energy; the experience of oneness.

Extension: The mode in which the soul expresses itself through unconditional love via the present, or eternal now.

Fifth-dimensional health: A high-vibrational state of being centered around the awareness of who you are spiritually, encompassing all aspects of being—mind, body, and soul; a reflection of spiritual embodiment.

Fifth-dimensional reality (5D): Also referred to as fifth-dimensional consciousness, 5D mind—the state of enlightenment; the experience of knowing through conscious awareness of inner stillness; oneness consciousness.

Fourth-dimensional reality (4D): Also referred to as fourth-dimensional consciousness—the bridge between third-dimensional reality and fifth-dimensional reality; an expanding awareness where one begins to question their beliefs.

Higher mind: The mind of Source.

Higher timeline: A more intentional and desired potential reality chosen through awareness, intention, and a shift of one's vibrational frequency. See timeline.

Highest self: The unseen, unmanifested self that is the source of the soul; Source or Source Energy.

I Am: The phrase that puts universal forces into action to call forth manifestation through the present moment; whatever follows "I am" is what one becomes energetically in the moment.

Infinite intelligence: The intelligence and life that is the source of all creation; also referred to as Source, Source Energy, or higher mind.

Inner being: The soul; your core, unmanifested essence that reflects stillness. See authentic self.

Inner guidance system: Your emotional inner compass and intuition combined; the information that comes from the subtle body, or soul, informing you when you're in or out of alignment.

Inner peace: A deep, profound sense of calm based in knowing and aligning with inner stillness.

Inner stillness: The reflection of the soul or inner being; the state of "no mind," where one is free of thought; cosmic or universal consciousness.

Intuition: The source of one's ability to know, sense, feel, and understand something using means beyond the five senses; clarity based in the third eye chakra, or sixth sense.

Invulnerability: An attribute of the soul and a state of mind that is fearless through conscious awareness of inner stillness; unharmable to reaction and negative emotion through centeredness.

Kundalini awakening: An activation of cosmic energy that includes third eye opening, which results in an inner shift from ego to universal, or cosmic, consciousness.

Law of Cancellation: The awareness of being able to negate fear, doubt, and frustration, as to be able to allow one's desires to come to fruition; this law is based in nonattachment and surrender.

Life: Source Energy expressing itself; Source becomes what Source creates; the creator and created are one.

Light body: The energetic body that connects the soul to the physical body; the body that houses the chakras. See subtle body.

Limiting belief: Any thought or idea that limits and contracts one's potential and possibility; any thought or attachment that lowers your energy field or vibrational frequency.

Mind-body: Refers to the connection between the mind (consciousness) and the physical body; as reflections of each other.

Negative thought: An idea or limiting energy sourced from the ego that is based in fear, anger, or any other low-vibrating energy that projects from the egoic mind.

New Earth: The clarity of seeing oneness—the spiritual nature of manifested reality, by first experiencing the dimension of inner stillness—one's own spiritual essence.

Nonlocal mind: The unbounded mind of Source; also referred to as the universal mind. See higher mind.

Oneness: The experience as a result of going beyond one's ego; the direct experience of inner stillness; the feeling and knowing that you are one with life, including everyone and everything—being one in mind, body, and spirit.

Potential: A spiritual faculty, ability, or experience that can be actualized through the cultivation of awareness.

Potential reality: One of countless realities that are available to be called forth from the unified field or unseen realm.

Projection: The mode in which the ego expresses itself through emotion via the past or the future.

Retrocognition: Having a knowing, deeper insight, or clarity about a past event using extrasensory perception.

Self: The inner being, multidimensional in nature, together with its level of wisdom, love, clarity, and understanding to feel and know.

Separation: In a spiritual sense, an experience based in the belief that one is separate from life, the outside world, including everyone and everything, including Source Energy.

Shadow work: The process of facing and transmuting our darker aspects—negative emotions—that have layered over us through our human conditioning.

Soul: See inner being.

Source: The All That Is; God, the source of all creation, the higher mind, also referred to as Source Energy. See infinite intelligence.

Source Energy: The unlimited, life-giving field of energy that is all-encompassing and omnipresent; the energy emanating from Source itself.

Spirit: The unmanifested, unseen essence of a human being; referring to one's true nature.

Spiritual realm: The unmanifested world encompassing the manifested world. See unified field.

Spiritual wellness: Knowing who you are spiritually and expressing that knowingness as awareness and a deep sense of purpose.

Sponsoring thought: An originating thought/belief that gives rise to other thoughts and emotions, positive or negative.

Stillness: See inner stillness.

Subtle body: The not completely spiritual, nor material, energetic body responsible for directing universal energy into the physical body through the chakras. See light body.

Supernatural Health: See fifth-dimensional health.

Surrender: The internal mental act of choosing to end inner conflict by aligning one's will with that of Source Energy; letting go, and allowing.

Third-dimensional reality (3D): Also referred to as third-dimensional consciousness—ego consciousness; an awareness that is strictly focused on the thinking mind; the initial starting point for every human being, and a catalyst for awakening.

Timeline: A current manifested reality, represented by one's past and current vibrational frequency. Different, even higher or desirable, timelines can be chosen through awareness, intention, and a shift of one's vibrational frequency.

Unconditional Love: The love of spirit, the core of one's inner being; the power behind all creation, love without attachment of any kind.

Unified field: From a spiritual point of view, the unseen, unmanifested world of spirit that surrounds the manifest world and everything in it; the birthplace for miracles, potential, and possibility.

Universal consciousness: See cosmic consciousness or inner stillness.

Universal energy: See cosmic energy.

Universal mind: The mind of Source. See nonlocal mind.

Vibrational frequency: The sum of one's thoughts, emotions, and out-look based on their level of awareness; refers to one's energy field.

Wholeness: An awareness that has integrated one's spiritual nature to being human; being one in mind, body, and spirit—the experience of oneness through stillness.

Zero-Point consciousness: The dimension of inner stillness; an expanded awareness where physical senses are heightened through the sixth sense, or third eye chakra.

To Write to the Author

If you wish to contact the author or would like more information about this book, please write to the author in care of Llewellyn Worldwide Ltd. and we will forward your request. Both the author and publisher appreciate hearing from you and learning of your enjoyment of this book and how it has helped you. Llewellyn Worldwide Ltd. cannot guarantee that every letter written to the author can be answered, but all will be forwarded. Please write to:

Jiulio Consiglio
℅ Llewellyn Worldwide
2143 Wooddale Drive
Woodbury, MN 55125-2989

Please enclose a self-addressed stamped envelope for reply,
or $1.00 to cover costs. If outside the U.S.A., enclose
an international postal reply coupon.

Many of Llewellyn's authors have websites with additional information and resources. For more information, please visit our website at http://www.llewellyn.com.